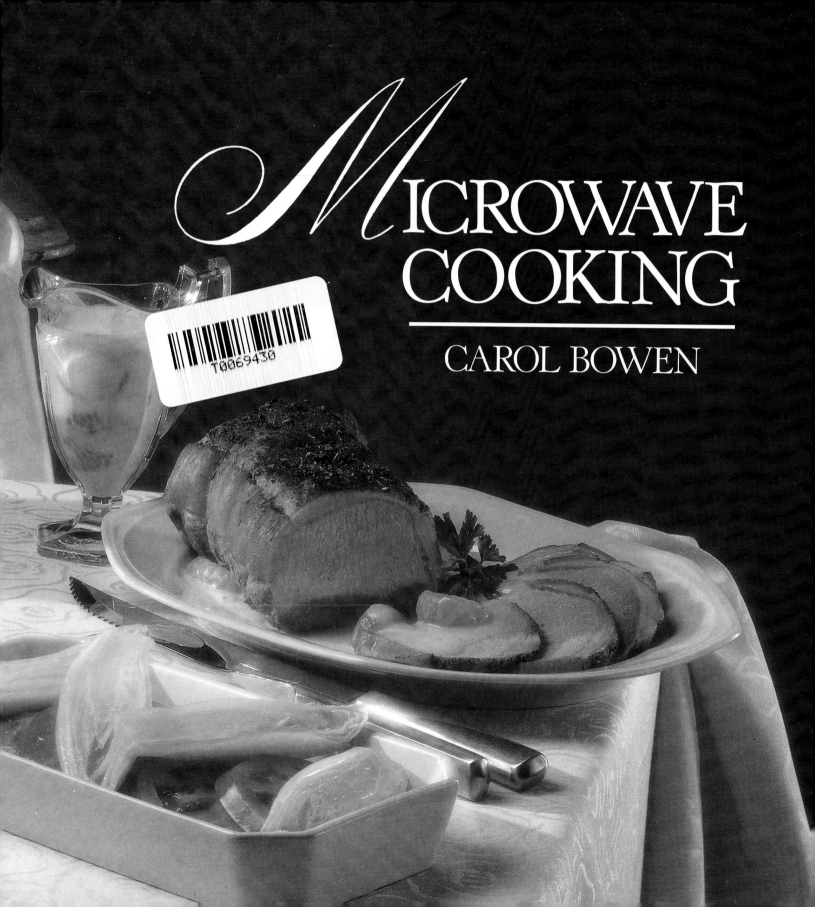

$\mathcal{M}$ICROWAVE COOKING

CAROL BOWEN

NOTE

1. All recipes serve four unless otherwise stated.

2. All spoon measurements are level. Spoon measures can be bought in both imperial and metric sizes to give accurate measurement of small quantities.

3. All eggs are size 2 or 3 unless otherwise stated.

4. All sugar is granulated unless otherwise stated.

5. Preparation times are an average calculated during recipe testing.

6. Metric and imperial measurements have been calculated separately. Use one set of measurements only as they are not exact equivalents.

7. Defrosting and cooking times may vary slightly depending on the output of the microwave cooker, the type and shape of container used and the temperature of the food. Therefore, always observe your manufacturer's instructions.

8. The recipes in this book were tested in a cooker with an output of 650-700 watts without a turntable using four power levels, Full, Medium, Defrost and Low. Food will need to be cooked for a few minutes longer in a cooker with a lower output.

9. All the recipes in this book have a variation for cooking in a combination microwave oven. They have been tested on a combination oven with a power rating of 600 watts.

10. When instructions have been given for using the combination oven in the microwave only mode, then automatic adjustment of times has been given to take into account the differing maximum power levels of the ovens used. If your combination microwave oven has a higher or lower maximum power wattage then follow the guidelines given above or in the manufacturer's handbook for time adjustments.

First published in 1988 by the Octopus Publishing Group
Michelin House, 81 Fulham Road, London SW3 6RB
© 1988 Hennerwood Publications Limited
Some of these recipes have previously appeared in
Complete Microwave Cookery,
originally published by Octopus Books Ltd in 1985
© 1985 Ridgmount Books Ltd

ISBN 0 86273 479 7
Printed in Italy

CONTENTS

SOUPS AND STARTERS

Whatever your choice, from thick nourishing soup for ladling, coarse-textured pâté for scooping to a creamy fondue or a piquant dip for dunking, here is a microwave cook's feast of delicious soups and starters to use in a wide range of menus. Serve with speedily-cooked microwave extras like warm bread rolls, hot crispy crackers or garlic bread for the perfect finishing touch.

Creamy carrot soup with croûtons (recipe, page 12)

MINI MEATBALLS WITH SPICED DIP

2 slices white bread
1 tablespoon milk
450 g (1 lb) minced beef
1 small onion, peeled and grated
2 teaspoons chopped fresh parsley
¼ teaspoon ground allspice
1 egg, beaten
salt
freshly ground black pepper

Dip:
8 tablespoons set plain unsweetened yogurt
   or mayonnaise
2 tablespoons finely chopped red pepper
3 tablespoons chilli relish
pinch of mild chilli powder
salt
freshly ground black pepper
1 tablespoon snipped fresh chives

Power setting: Full/Maximum
Preparation and cooking time: 15–20
minutes

1. Cut the crusts from the white bread and discard them. Soak the bread in the milk, gently squeeze dry, then mix with the minced beef. Add the grated onion, parsley, allspice, beaten egg and season with salt and pepper to taste, then beat well to bind the mixture together. Shape the mixture into about 20 small meatballs.
2. Place the meatballs in a shallow cooking dish, in a ring pattern if possible. Cook, uncovered, for 6–8 minutes, rotating the dish and turning the meatballs over twice. Allow to stand for 2 minutes.
3. Meanwhile, to make the dip, gently mix together the unsweetened yogurt or

mayonnaise with the red pepper, chilli relish, chilli powder and season with salt and pepper. Spoon the dip into a small bowl, garnish it with the snipped chives and place it on a large warmed serving plate. Surround the bowl with the hot meatballs and serve with cocktail sticks.

COMBINATION OVENS:
Prepare and cook as above using *microwave only* but increase the cooking time in Step 2 to 7–9½ minutes.

PRAWN AND WATERCRESS SOUP

25 g (1 oz) butter
1 large bunch watercress, washed and
   trimmed
1 onion, peeled and thinly sliced
225 g (8 oz) frozen peas
600 ml (1 pint) milk
salt
freshly ground black pepper
150 ml (¼ pint) single cream
100 g (4 oz) peeled prawns, chopped

To garnish:
sprigs of watercress
4 whole prawns

Power setting: Full/Maximum
Preparation and cooking time: 20–25
minutes, plus chilling

1. Place the butter, watercress and onion in a large bowl. Cover and cook for 3 minutes, stirring once.
2. Add the peas and half of the milk. Cover and cook for 10 minutes, stirring once.
3. Purée in a blender or pass through a fine sieve with the remaining milk. Season to taste with salt and pepper. Chill thoroughly.
4. Whisk the cream into the soup and stir in the prawns. Serve chilled, garnished with watercress sprigs and whole prawns.

COMBINATION OVENS:
Prepare and cook as above using *microwave only* but increase the cooking times in Step 1 to 3½ minutes and Step 2 to 12 minutes.

Although there is no waste with vacuum packed watercress, bunches are a better buy when you are making soup; they contain more stalk and this adds body and flavour. When you get bunches of watercress home, trim the stalks, pick over the leaves, rinse, pack into polythene bags, pressing out as much air as possible and store in the salad drawer of the refrigerator.

FROM THE LEFT: Prawn and watercress soup; Mini meatballs with spiced dip

SOMERSET CIDERED FONDUE

½ garlic clove, peeled
250 ml (8 fl oz) dry Somerset cider
1 teaspoon lemon juice
400 g (14 oz) Cheshire or Cheddar cheese, grated
1 tablespoon cornflour
salt
freshly ground black pepper
1 medium French stick, cubed, to serve

Power setting: Full/Maximum and Medium
Preparation and cooking time: 10 minutes

If your fondue dish is not suitable for use in the microwave, cook the fondue in another dish and transfer for serving.
1. Rub the inside of a fondue dish with the cut side of the garlic.
2. Add the cider and the lemon juice. Cover and cook on full/maximum power for 2–3 minutes until the mixture is very hot, but not boiling.
3. Toss the cheese with the cornflour and salt and pepper to taste, and quickly stir or whisk it into the hot cider mixture. Reduce the power setting to medium and cook for 4–4½ minutes, until smooth, hot and melted, stirring every 1 minute.
4. Place the dish over a spirit burner and serve at once with small cubes of crusty bread, speared with fondue forks.

COMBINATION OVENS:
Prepare and cook as above using *microwave only* but increase the cooking times in Step 2 on full/maximum power to 2½–3½ minutes and Step 3 on medium power to 4½–5½ minutes.

MULLIGATAWNY SOUP

25 g (1 oz) butter
1 onion, peeled and chopped
1 carrot, peeled and chopped
2 celery sticks, scrubbed and chopped
½ green pepper, cored, seeded and chopped
225 g (8 oz) tomatoes, peeled and chopped
1 apple, peeled, cored and chopped
900 ml (1½ pints) boiling stock
1 tablespoon curry powder
2 cloves
1 tablespoon chopped fresh parsley
1 tablespoon sugar
salt
freshly ground black pepper
2 tablespoons cornflour
150 ml (¼ pint) milk
75–100 g (3–4 oz) cooked lamb, beef or chicken, finely chopped
25 g (1 oz) long-grain rice

Power setting: Full/Maximum
Preparation and cooking time: 40–45 minutes

1. Place the butter, onion, carrot, celery and pepper in a large bowl. Cover and cook for 4 minutes, stirring once.
2. Add the tomatoes and apple, blending well. Cover and cook for 2 minutes.
3. Add the stock, curry powder, cloves, parsley, sugar and salt and pepper to taste. Cover and cook for 10 minutes, stirring once.
4. Blend the cornflour with a little of the milk then stir in the remaining milk. Stir into the soup with the meat and rice. Cook, uncovered, for 8 minutes, stirring twice. Cover and leave to stand for 5 minutes or until the rice is tender.
5. Cook for 2 minutes to reheat for serving.

FREEZING DETAILS
1. Prepare the recipe to the end of Step 4.
2. Cool quickly, transfer to a rigid container, allowing 2.5 cm (1 inch) headspace. Cover, seal, label and freeze for up to 1 month.

REHEATING DETAILS
Power setting: Full/Maximum
Defrosting and cooking time: 18–22 minutes
1. Remove all wrappings and place the frozen soup in a serving tureen. Cook for 18–22 minutes, breaking up the soup and stirring every 5 minutes. Serve hot.

COMBINATION OVENS:
Prepare and cook as above using *microwave only* but increase the cooking times in Step 1 to 5 minutes; Step 2 to 2½ minutes; Step 3 to 12 minutes; Step 4 to 9½ minutes and Step 5 to 2½ minutes.
Reheating details: Follow the instructions above using *microwave only* but increase the cooking times in Step 1 to 21–25 minutes.

FROM THE TOP: Somerset cidered fondue; Mulligatawny soup

CREAMY CARROT SOUP WITH CROÛTONS

25 g (1 oz) butter
450 g (1 lb) carrots, peeled and sliced
225 g (8 oz) onions, peeled and sliced
½ small red pepper, cored, seeded and
  sliced
600 ml (1 pint) boiling vegetable or chicken
  stock
salt
freshly ground black pepper
150 ml (¼ pint) single cream

Croûtons:
25 g (1 oz) butter
175 g (6 oz) bread, crusts removed and cut
  into 1 cm (½ inch) cubes
2 teaspoons chopped fresh herbs

Power setting: Full/Maximum
Preparation and cooking time: 30–35
minutes

1. Place the butter, carrots, onions and red pepper in a large bowl. Cover and cook for 12–14 minutes, stirring twice.
2. Add the stock and salt and pepper to taste. Cover and cook for 3–5 minutes or until the vegetables are tender.
3. Purée the vegetables in a blender or pass them through a fine sieve and return them to a bowl. Stir in the cream and cook for 3–5 minutes to reheat. Leave the soup to stand, covered, while you are preparing the croûtons.
4. Place the butter in a large shallow dish and cook for 30 seconds. Add the bread cubes and herbs and toss to coat. Cook for 3–4 minutes, stirring every 1 minute.
5. Serve the soup sprinkled with the herby croûtons.

FREEZING DETAILS.
1. Prepare the recipe to the end of Step 2.
2. Purée the soup in a blender or pass through a fine sieve. Cool quickly, transfer to a rigid container, allowing 2.5 cm (1 inch) headspace. Cover, seal, label and freeze for up to 3 months.

REHEATING DETAILS
Power setting: Full/Maximum
Defrosting and cooking time: 16–19 minutes

1. Remove all wrappings and place the frozen soup in a serving tureen. Cook for 14–17 minutes, breaking up the soup and stirring every 3 minutes.
2. Stir in the cream and cook for 2 minutes to reheat. Leave to stand, covered, while preparing the croûtons as in Step 4 above.

COMBINATION OVENS:
Prepare and cook as in Steps 1–5, using *microwave only* but increase the cooking times in Step 1 to 14–16½ minutes; Step 2 to 3½–6 minutes; Step 3 to 3½–6 minutes and Step 4 to 3½-4½ minutes.
Reheating details: Follow the instructions above using *microwave only* but increase the cooking times in Step 1 to 16½–20 minutes and Step 2 to 2½ minutes.

BORTSCH

500–750 g (1¼–1½ lb) raw beetroot, peeled
  and finely grated
900 ml (1½ pints) boiling water
1½ teaspoons salt
¼ teaspoon freshly ground black pepper
25 g (1 oz) sugar
4½ tablespoons lemon juice
150 ml (¼ pint) soured cream

Power setting: Full/Maximum
Preparation and cooking time: 20–25
minutes, plus chilling

1. Place the grated beetroot, water, salt, pepper, sugar and lemon juice in a large bowl. Cook, uncovered, for 14–16 minutes, stirring twice, or until the beetroot is quite tender.
2. Cover and leave to cool, then chill for 4–6 hours or overnight.
3. Spoon the soup into serving bowls and top each one with a spoonful of soured cream. Serve chilled.

COMBINATION OVENS:
Prepare and cook as above using *microwave only* but increase the cooking times in Step 1 to 16½–18½ minutes.

FROM THE TOP: Creamy carrot soup with croûtons; Bortsch

MUSSEL CHOWDER

100 g (4 oz) unsmoked streaky bacon,
  rinded and chopped
1 onion, peeled and chopped
1 celery stick, scrubbed and chopped
1 small green pepper, cored, seeded and
  chopped
2 small potatoes, peeled and chopped
450 ml (¾ pint) boiling water
1 bay leaf
salt
freshly ground black pepper
40 g (1½ oz) plain flour
600 ml (1 pint) milk
275 g (10 oz) cooked mussels, drained
chopped fresh parsley, to garnish

Power setting: Full/Maximum
Preparation and cooking time: 30–35
minutes

1. Place the bacon in a large bowl. Cook for 2 minutes, stirring once.
2. Add the onion, celery and green pepper and cook for 3 minutes, stirring once.
3. Add the potatoes, water, bay leaf and salt and pepper to taste. Cover and cook for 6 minutes, stirring once. Remove and discard the bay leaf.
4. Blend the flour with a little of the milk, then add the remaining milk. Whisk the milk mixture into the soup. Cook, uncovered, for 10 minutes, whisking every 2 minutes.
5. Add the mussels and cook for a further 3 minutes, stirring once.
6. Serve hot sprinkled with chopped parsley to garnish.

COMBINATION OVENS:
Prepare and cook as above using *microwave only* but increase the cooking times in Step 1 to 2½ minutes; Step 2 to 3½ minutes; Step 3 to 7 minutes; Step 4 to 12 minutes and Step 5 to 3½ minutes.

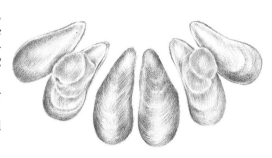

MONKFISH APPETIZER

SERVES 4–6
450 g (1 lb) monkfish, boned and cut into
  bite-sized pieces
3 oranges, peeled, pith removed and
  segmented
3 grapefruit, peeled, pith removed and
  segmented
1 honeydew melon, peeled, seeded and
  scooped into balls, saving the juice
2 carrots, peeled and grated

Dressing:
1 medium mango, peeled and stoned
1 banana, peeled
1–2 tablespoons white rum
pinch of ground nutmeg

Power setting: Full/Maximum
Preparation and cooking time: 10–15
minutes

1. Place the monkfish in a shallow dish and sprinkle over a little of the reserved fruit juice. Cover and cook for 3–4 minutes, stirring twice. Allow to cool.
2. Mix the monkfish with the oranges, grapefruit, melon and carrot, blending well.
3. To make the dressing, place the mango, banana, rum and nutmeg in a blender and purée until smooth.
4. Divide the fish and fruit mixture between individual serving glasses and spoon over the dressing. Serve lightly chilled.

COMBINATION OVENS:
Prepare and cook as above using *microwave only* but increase the cooking time in Step 1 to 3½–4½ minutes.

Monkfish is a deep-sea fish that you are unlikely to see for sale whole. It has a very heavy, ugly head so usually just the tailpiece is sold. The flesh is white, firm and succulent and not unlike scampi. Your fishmonger will generally remove the flesh from the tail piece, but should you wish to do this, then slice on either side of the central bone to remove the two fillets, then slice or cube as desired.

FROM THE TOP: Mussel chowder; Monkfish appetizer

BAGNA CAUDA

250 ml (8 fl oz) double cream
15 g (½ oz) butter
1–2 garlic cloves, peeled and crushed
25–50 g (1–2 oz) anchovy fillets, mashed
½ teaspoon salt
pinch of dried mixed herbs
pinch of sugar
freshly ground black pepper

To serve:
vegetable crudités, for example, celery
  sticks, carrot sticks, cauliflower florets,
  cherry tomatoes, button mushrooms, spring
  onions, courgette sticks, lettuce wedges or
  mangetout
bread sticks

Power setting: Full/Maximum and
Medium
Preparation and cooking time: 10–15
minutes

This is a mild variation of the robust anchovy and garlic dip which is a speciality of Piedmont in northern Italy. If you want a stronger version, add more garlic and anchovy fillets.

1. Place the cream in a large jug and cook on full/maximum power for 3–4 minutes until boiling, bubbly and thickened.
2. Place the butter, garlic and anchovies in a bowl and cook on full/maximum power for 1½ minutes. Stir in the salt, herbs, sugar and hot cream, blending well. Cook on medium power for 2–4 minutes until hot, creamy and well blended, stirring twice.
3. Place the bagna cauda in a small bowl on a large serving platter, sprinkle with black pepper and surround with vegetable crudités and bread sticks for dipping. Serve at once while still warm.

COMBINATION OVENS:
Prepare and cook as above using *microwave only* but increase the cooking times in Step 1 on full/maximum power to 3½–4½ minutes and Step 2 on full/maximum power to 1½–2 minutes then medium power to 2½–4½ minutes.

BRANDIED CHICKEN LIVER PÂTÉ

SERVES 6
25 g (1 oz) butter
1 small onion, peeled and chopped
1 x 225 g (8 oz) carton frozen chicken
  livers, thawed, rinsed and trimmed
200 g (7 oz) wholemeal bread, cubed
150 ml (¼ pint) milk
3 tablespoons chopped fresh parsley
1 egg yolk
1 tablespoon brandy
salt
freshly ground black pepper
200 g (7 oz) uncooked chicken breast,
  skinned and cut into thin strips
oak lettuce, to garnish

Power setting: Full/Maximum and
Medium
Preparation and cooking time: about
30 minutes, plus chilling

1. Place the butter in a bowl and cook on full/maximum power for 30 seconds.
2. Add the onion and livers, blending well. Cover and cook on full/maximum power for 2½ minutes, stirring once.
3. Meanwhile, place the bread cubes in a bowl and pour over the milk.
4. Place the liver mixture, bread, 1 tablespoon of the parsley, egg yolk, brandy and salt and pepper to taste in a blender and purée until finely chopped.
5. Line the base of a 1 litre (1¾ pint) loaf dish with greaseproof paper. Spoon in one-third of the liver mixture and level the surface. Cover with a layer of half of the chicken breast and half the remaining parsley. Cover this with another third of the liver mixture and then a final layer of chicken breast and parsley. Top with the remaining liver mixture and press down.

6. Cover and cook on medium power for 17–18 minutes, or until the pâté in the centre of the terrine is just firm to the touch. Leave to stand, covered, for 10 minutes, then cool quickly and chill thoroughly for 2 hours.
7. The pâté may be turned out on to a plate or sliced from the dish. Garnish with oak lettuce and serve with toast.

COMBINATION OVENS:
Prepare and cook as above using *microwave only* but increase the cooking times in Step 2 on full/maximum power to 3 minutes and Step 6 on medium power to 20–21 minutes.

FROM THE TOP: Bagna cauda; Brandied chicken liver pâté

VEGETABLES

Brightly-coloured, tender-crisp and bursting with all their vitamins, vegetables cooked in the microwave have the edge on their conventionally boiled, steamed or baked cousins – but remember to allow a little standing time at the end of cooking for perfect results. Serve the recipes that follow as accompaniments to a main meal dish, rustle up a selection for a vegetarian feast or make just one as an inexpensive starter to a seasonal menu.

Provençale vegetables (recipe, page 26)

GREEN BEANS IN TANGY TOMATO SAUCE

1 small onion, peeled and finely chopped
1 garlic clove, peeled and crushed
2 rashers unsmoked back bacon, rinded and
  chopped
1 x 225 g (8 oz) can peeled tomatoes
1 teaspoon dried mixed herbs
pinch of sugar
1 x 275 g (10 oz) packet frozen whole green
  beans

Power setting: Full/Maximum
Preparation and cooking time: about
20 minutes

1. Place the onion, garlic and bacon in a medium cooking dish. Cook for 2 minutes, stirring once.
2. Add the tomatoes with their juice, the herbs, sugar and frozen beans, blending well. Cover and cook for 10 minutes, stirring twice.
3. Leave to stand, covered, for 3 minutes before serving.

COMBINATION OVENS:
Prepare and cook as above using *microwave only* but increase the cooking times in Step 1 to 2–2½ minutes and in Step 2 to 11½–12 minutes.

BRAISED FENNEL WITH HAM AND CHEESE SAUCE

450 g (1 lb) fennel, trimmed and halved,
  leaves reserved for garnish
300 ml (½ pint) water
salt
2 tablespoons plain flour
4 tablespoons cold water
50 g (2 oz) cooked ham, chopped
50 g (2 oz) Cheddar or Double Gloucester
  cheese, grated
freshly ground black pepper
2–3 tablespoons soured cream

Power setting: Full/Maximum and
Medium
Preparation and cooking time: about
35 minutes

1. Place the fennel, cut sides down, in a cooking dish. Add the water and a pinch of salt. Cover and cook on full/maximum power for 5 minutes.
2. Turn the fennel over, re–cover, reduce the power setting to medium and cook for a further 15–20 minutes, until tender. Remove the fennel with a slotted spoon and set aside.
3. Mix the flour and cold water to a smooth paste and stir into the hot fennel stock. Stir in the ham, cheese and pepper to taste, blending well. Cook on full/maximum power for 2 minutes, stirring twice.
4. Add the fennel and soured cream, tossing well so that the fennel is coated in the sauce. Cook on full/maximum power for 2 minutes. Serve hot, garnished with the reserved fennel leaves.

COMBINATION OVENS:
Prepare and cook as above using *microwave only* but increase the cooking times in Step 1 on full/maximum power to 6 minutes; Step 2 on medium power to 17½–23½ minutes; Step 3 on full/maximum power to 2–2½ minutes and Step 4 on full/maximum power to 2–2½ minutes.

Fennel, also known as Florence fennel and finocchio, is a bulbous vegetable with a crisp ribbed texture, not unlike celery. However, unlike celery, it has a distinctive aniseed or liquorice flavour. The swollen bulb can be eaten raw or cooked, while the feathery green leaves make an attractive garnish.

FROM THE TOP: Green beans in tangy tomato sauce; Braised fennel with ham and cheese sauce

HUNGARIAN STUFFED PEPPERS

1 tablespoon oil
1 onion, peeled and chopped
1 garlic clove, peeled and crushed
450 g (1 lb) lean minced beef
1 tablespoon tomato purée
1 tablespoon paprika
100 g (4 oz) long–grain rice
350 ml (12 fl oz) boiling water
salt
freshly ground black pepper
4 large green, yellow or red peppers
soured cream, to serve

To garnish:
sprigs of thyme
celery leaves

Power setting: Full/Maximum and Medium
Preparation and cooking time: about 40 minutes, plus standing

1. Place the oil, onion and garlic in a bowl. Cover and cook on full/maximum power for 2 minutes. Stir in the beef. Cover and cook on full/maximum power for 5 minutes, stirring to break up twice.
2. Add the tomato purée, paprika, rice, boiling water and salt and pepper to taste, blending well. Cover and cook on full/maximum power for 5 minutes. Stir well, reduce the power setting to medium and cook for a further 10 minutes, stirring twice.
3. Using a sharp knife, cut a slice from the stalk end of each pepper and remove the core and seeds.
4. Stand the peppers upright snugly in a large dish and fill each equally with the goulash mixture. Cover and cook on full/maximum power for 8–10 minutes, re-arranging once. Leave to stand for 5 minutes. Serve topped with a little soured cream and garnish with sprigs of thyme and celery leaves.

FREEZING DETAILS
1. Prepare the recipe to the end of Step 4.
2. Cool quickly, cover, seal, label and freeze for up to 3 months.

REHEATING DETAILS
Power setting: Defrost and Full/Maximum
Defrosting and reheating time: 30 minutes
1. Remove all wrappings and cook on defrost power for 25 minutes.
2. Cook on full/maximum power for 5 minutes to reheat.

COMBINATION OVENS:
Prepare and cook as above using *microwave only* to the end of Step 3 but increase the cooking times in Step 1 on full/maximum power to 2½ minutes, then 6 minutes and Step 2 on full/maximum power to 6 minutes, then medium for 11½ minutes. Stuff the peppers with the goulash mixture and *combination bake* at 200°C using *medium* power for 10–15 minutes.
Reheating details: Follow the instructions above using *microwave only* but increase the cooking times in Step 1 on defrost power to 30 minutes and Step 2 on full/maximum power to 6 minutes.

CHEESY STUFFED MUSHROOMS

225 g (8 oz) large cap or flat mushrooms, wiped
15 g (½ oz) butter
¼ small onion, peeled and finely chopped
50 g (2 oz) salami, garlic sausage or other delicatessen meat, finely chopped
50 g (2 oz) Cheddar cheese, grated
2 tablespoons breadcrumbs
salad leaves, to garnish (optional)

Power setting: Full/Maximum
Preparation and cooking time: 10 minutes

1. Remove the stalks from the mushrooms and chop them finely.
2. Place the butter, chopped mushroom stalks and onion in a bowl and cook for 2 minutes, stirring once.
3. Add the chopped salami or other delicatessen meat, blending well. Mound the stuffing evenly into the mushroom caps.
4. Mix the cheese with the breadcrumbs and sprinkle over the stuffing mixture. Arrange in a shallow cooking dish and cook for 2½–3 minutes, rearranging once. Serve hot with a salad garnish, if liked.

COMBINATION OVENS:
Prepare and cook as above using *microwave only* to the end of Step 3. Mix the cheese with the breadcrumbs and sprinkle over the stuffing mixture. Arrange in a shallow cooking dish and *combination bake* at 250°C using *medium* power for 5–7 minutes.

FROM THE LEFT: Hungarian stuffed peppers; Cheesy stuffed mushrooms

FRUITY POTATO SALAD

8 rashers unsmoked back bacon, rinded
450 g (1 lb) new potatoes, scrubbed
4 tablespoons water
4 spring onions, trimmed and finely sliced
1 x 200 g (7 oz) can sweetcorn kernels,
  drained
100 g (4 oz) black grapes, halved and
  seeded
50 g (2 oz) no-need-to-soak dried apricots,
  chopped
lettuce leaves, to serve

Dressing:
100 g (4 oz) Danish blue cheese, rinded
2 tablespoons mayonnaise
3 tablespoons single cream or thick set plain
  unsweetened yogurt
2 tablespoons milk
salt
freshly ground black pepper

Power setting: Full/Maximum
Preparation and cooking time: about
30 minutes, plus chilling

1. Place the bacon on a plate or bacon rack
and cover with paper towels. Cook for 6–8
minutes until cooked and crisp, turning
over once. Allow to cool, then crumble or
cut into bite-sized pieces.
2. Place the potatoes in a bowl with the
water. Cover and cook for 6–8 minutes,
stirring once. Leave to stand, covered, for
5 minutes, then drain and thickly slice or
cut into cubes.
3. Mix the bacon with the potatoes, spring
onions, sweetcorn, grapes and apricots,
blending well.

4. Meanwhile, soften the cheese in a bowl.
Gradually beat in the mayonnaise, single
cream or yogurt and milk, and add salt and
pepper to taste.
5. Spoon the dressing over the potato salad
and toss gently to coat. Chill lightly before
serving on a bed of lettuce.

COMBINATION OVENS:
Prepare and cook as above using *microwave only* but increase the cooking times in
Step 1 to 7–9½ minutes and Step 2 to
7–9½ minutes.

FRESH ASPARAGUS WITH HERBED BUTTER SAUCE

450 g (1 lb) fresh asparagus
125 ml (4½ fl oz) water
100 g (4 oz) butter
4 tablespoons finely chopped fresh herbs,
  e.g. chives, parsley and tarragon
salt
freshly ground black pepper
twists of lemon or lime, to garnish

Power setting: Full/Maximum
Preparation and cooking time: about
20 minutes

*FROM THE LEFT: Fresh asparagus with herbed
butter sauce; Fruity potato salad*

1. Trim the woody ends from the asparagus and thinly pare the outer tough skin
from the stalk. Arrange in a shallow cooking dish with the pointed tips to the
centre. Add the water, cover and cook for
12–14 minutes, rearranging the spears, but
still keeping the tips to the centre, halfway
through the cooking time, until tender.
Drain and place on a warmed serving dish.
2. Place the butter in a bowl. Cover and
cook for 1½–2 minutes until melted and
bubbling hot. Stir in the herbs and salt and
pepper to taste, blending well.
3. Spoon over the asparagus, garnish, and
serve at once.

COMBINATION OVENS:
Prepare and cook as above using *microwave only* but increase the cooking times in
Step 1 to 14–16½ minutes and in Step 2 to
1¾–2½ minutes.

POTATOES LYONNAISE

25 g (1 oz) butter
1 small onion, peeled and chopped or small
  bunch of spring onions, trimmed and
  chopped
750 g (1½ lb) potatoes, peeled and thinly
  sliced
1 garlic clove, peeled and crushed
salt
freshly ground black pepper
200 ml (7 fl oz) single cream or milk
snipped chives, to garnish

Power setting: Full/Maximum
Preparation and cooking time: about
20–25 minutes

1. Place the butter in a 20 cm (8 inch) shallow flameproof dish and cook for ½ minute to melt. Brush around the dish to coat.
2. Layer the onions, potatoes and garlic in the dish, seasoning between each layer with salt and pepper to taste, and finishing with a potato layer.
3. Pour over the cream or milk, cover and cook for 7 minutes.
4. Remove the cover and cook for a further 7–9 minutes, giving the dish a half–turn twice. Leave to stand for 5 minutes.
5. Brown under a preheated hot grill before serving, if liked. Serve sprinkled with snipped chives.

COMBINATION OVENS:
Prepare and cook as above using *microwave only* to the end of Step 2. Pour over the cream or milk and *combination bake*, uncovered, at 180° C using *high* power for 16–20 minutes, until the potatoes are tender and the top is crisp and golden. Garnish with snipped chives to serve.

This is a very popular dinner party treat, but so simple to prepare that it could be an everyday dish as well. For best results, choose a potato like Maris Piper or Croft.

PROVENÇALE VEGETABLES

SERVES 4–6
3 tablespoons olive oil
1 onion, peeled and thinly sliced
1 garlic clove, peeled and crushed
1 carrot, peeled and cut into thin strips
1 small green pepper, cored, seeded and
  sliced
350 g (12 oz) aubergines, cubed, sprinkled
  with salt and left to drain for 30 minutes
225 g (8 oz) courgettes, trimmed and sliced
¼ cauliflower, broken into small florets
2 tomatoes, cut into thin wedges
1 teaspoon dried basil
1 teaspoon dried mixed herbs
50 g (2 oz) tiny button mushrooms, wiped
salt
freshly ground black pepper

Power setting: Full/Maximum
Preparation and cooking time: about
30 minutes

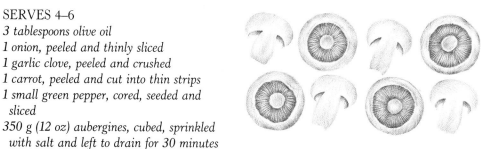

1. Place the oil, onion and garlic in a large casserole dish. Cook for 4 minutes, stirring once.
2. Add the carrot and green pepper, blending well. Rinse the aubergines and pat dry with paper towels. Add to the onion mixture with the courgettes and cauliflower. Cover and cook for 4 minutes, stirring once.
3. Add the tomatoes, basil, dried herbs, mushrooms and salt and pepper to taste, blending well. Cook, uncovered, for 4 minutes, stirring once, until just tender.
4. Serve hot or cold as a starter or vegetable dish.

COMBINATION OVENS:
Prepare and cook as above using *microwave only* but increase the cooking times in Step 1 to 4½–4¾ minutes; Step 2 to 4½–4¾ minutes and Step 3 to 4½–4¾ minutes.

FROM THE TOP: Potatoes Lyonnaise; Provençale vegetables

BROCCOLI WITH BACON AND YOGURT SAUCE

750 g (1½ lb) broccoli spears
6 tablespoons water
8 rashers unsmoked back bacon, rinded
40 g (1½ oz) butter
40 g (1½ oz) plain flour
450 ml (¾ pint) milk
150 ml (¼ pint) plain unsweetened yogurt
freshly ground black pepper
2 tablespoons chopped red pepper, to
  garnish

Power setting: Full/Maximum
Preparation and cooking time: 25–30
minutes

1. Place the broccoli spears in a large shallow dish with the heads to the centre of the dish. Add the water, cover and cook for 10–12 minutes until tender. Leave the broccoli to stand, covered, while preparing the sauce.

2. Place the bacon on a plate or bacon rack and cover with paper towels. Cook for 6–7 minutes, turning over once. Cut the rashers into quarters.
3. Place the butter in a large jug and cook for 1 minute to melt. Blend in the flour and milk and cook for 4–4½ minutes, stirring every minute until the mixture is smooth and thick. Add the yogurt and three–quarters of the bacon. Season with pepper to taste and blend well.
4. Drain the broccoli and arrange it in a shallow serving dish. Spoon over the sauce and sprinkle with the remaining bacon and the red pepper to garnish.

COMBINATION OVENS:
Prepare and cook as above using *microwave only* but increase the cooking times in Step 1 to 11½–14 minutes; Step 2 to 7–8 minutes and Step 3 to 1¼ minutes, then 4½–5¼ minutes.

STUFFED TOMATOES

4 large tomatoes
25 g (1 oz) butter
1 garlic clove, peeled and crushed
75 g (3 oz) fresh breadcrumbs
50 g (2 oz) freshly grated Parmesan cheese
3 tablespoons finely chopped fresh parsley
salt
freshly ground black pepper
sprigs of parsley, to garnish

Power setting: Full/Maximum
Preparation and cooking time: about 10
minutes

1. Remove the tops from the tomatoes, scoop out and discard the seeds. Stand upside down on paper towels to drain.
2. Place the butter in a bowl and cook for ½ minute to melt. Add the garlic and cook for 1 minute.
3. Stir in the breadcrumbs, cheese, parsley and salt and pepper to taste. Spoon the mixture evenly into the tomato cases. Stand upright in a small baking dish. Cook for 2 minutes, turning the dish or rearranging the tomatoes once, until just tender. Leave to stand for 2 minutes before serving, garnished with sprigs of parsley.

COMBINATION OVENS:
Prepare and cook as above using *microwave only* but increase the cooking times in Step 2 to ½–¾ minute, then 1–1¼ minutes and Step 3 to 2–2½ minutes.

FROM THE TOP: Broccoli with bacon and yogurt sauce; Stuffed tomatoes

BRUSSELS SPROUTS WITH HORSERADISH

275 g (10 oz) frozen Brussels sprouts
4 tablespoons water
1 tablespoon horseradish sauce
2 tablespoons single cream
salt
freshly ground black pepper
sprigs of parsley, to garnish

Power setting: Full/Maximum
Preparation and cooking time: 15 minutes

1. Place the frozen Brussels sprouts in a medium cooking dish with the water. Cover and cook for **7** minutes, stirring once. Drain thoroughly.
2. Mix the horseradish sauce with the cream and stir into the sprouts. Cook for 1 minute. Season with salt and pepper to taste, garnish and serve.

COMBINATION OVENS:
Prepare and cook as above using *micro-wave only* but increase the cooking times in Step 1 to 8–8¼ minutes and Step 2 to 1–1¼ minutes.

CHICORY WITH TOMATOES

350 g (12 oz) tomatoes, thickly sliced
salt
freshly ground black pepper
50 g (2 oz) butter
450 g (1 lb) chicory, trimmed and halved
1 teaspoon cornflour
2 tablespoons single cream

Power setting: Full/Maximum and Medium
Preparation and cooking time: about 25 minutes

1. Place the tomatoes in a greased cooking dish. Season with salt and pepper to taste. Dot with the butter.
2. Arrange the chicory halves on top and season with salt to taste. Cover and cook on full/maximum power for 10 minutes, giving the dish a half-turn once.
3. Reduce the power setting to medium and cook for a further 5 minutes.
4. Mix the cornflour with the cream and stir into the vegetable mixture, blending well. Cook on full/maximum power for 2–3 minutes. Serve at once.

COMBINATION OVENS:
Prepare and cook as above using *micro-wave only* but increase the cooking times in Step 2 on full/maximum power to 11½ minutes; Step 3 on medium power to 6 minutes and Step 4 on full/maximum power to 2½–3½ minutes.

CORN-ON-THE-COB WITH GARLIC BUTTER

100 g (4 oz) butter
2 garlic cloves, peeled and crushed
4 x 175–225 g (6–8 oz) fresh corn-on-the-cobs, husked
salt
freshly ground black pepper
sprigs of thyme, to garnish

Power setting: Full/Maximum
Preparation and cooking time: about 15–20 minutes

1. Mix the butter with the garlic, blending well. Spread evenly over the corn-on-the-cobs.
2. Place in a shallow cooking dish, cover and cook for 9–10 minutes, turning over and rearranging once. Leave to stand, covered, for 3–5 minutes.
3. Season with salt and pepper to taste, garnish, and serve hot.

COMBINATION OVENS:
Prepare and cook as above using *micro-wave only* but increase the cooking time in Step 2 to 10½–11 mintues.

CLOCKWISE FROM THE TOP: Brussels sprouts with horseradish; Corn-on-the-cob with garlic butter; Chicory with tomatoes

TOMATO AND COURGETTE QUICHE

Pastry:
175 g (6 oz) plain white or wholemeal flour
pinch of salt
75 g (3 oz) butter or margarine
2 tablespoons iced water

Filling:
3 courgettes, trimmed and sliced
175 g (6 oz) sliced tomatoes
75 g (3 oz) Cheddar cheese, grated
2 eggs, beaten
150 ml (¼ pint) milk
salt
freshly ground black pepper

Power setting: Full/Maximum, Medium and Defrost
Preparation and cooking time: about 40–45 minutes, plus standing

Most manufacturers of combination microwave ovens claim that a quiche does not need to be baked 'blind' before filling and combination baking. However, with some extra 'wet' fillings a short pre-cooking period is advisable. To bake a quiche 'blind' in a combination oven, line the quiche with foil or greaseproof paper and ceramic baking beans. Do not line the dish with absorbent paper towels as you would with a basic microwave cooker as they will burn because of the high temperature, as in a conventional oven. Cook by convection only at 200°C for 10–15 minutes.

1. To make the pastry, mix the flour with the salt in a bowl. Rub in the butter or margarine until the mixture resembles fine breadcrumbs. Add the water and bind together to a firm but pliable dough. Turn the pastry on to a lightly floured surface and knead until it is smooth and free from cracks.
2. Roll out the pastry on a lightly floured surface to make a round large enough to line a 20 cm (8 inch) flan dish. Press it in firmly, taking care not to stretch the pastry. Cut away the excess pastry, leaving a 5 mm (¼ inch) 'collar' above the dish to allow for any shrinkage that may occur during cooking. Prick the base and sides of the quiche well with a fork.
3. Place a double thickness layer of paper towel over the base, easing it into position round the edges.
4. Cook on full/maximum power for 3½ minutes, giving the dish a quarter–turn every 1 minute. Remove the paper and cook on full/maximum power for a further 1½–2 minutes, until the pastry case is fully cooked.
5. Place the courgettes in a bowl, cover and cook them for 2–3 minutes, shaking the bowl once. Drain thoroughly and place in the base of the quiche with the tomatoes and cheese.
6. Mix the eggs with the milk and salt and pepper to taste. Cook on medium power for 3–4 minutes or until hot, stirring once – the mixture may thicken slightly at this stage. Spoon into the flan case and cook on defrost power for 14–16 minutes, giving the dish a quarter turn every 3 minutes. The quiche is cooked when a knife inserted halfway between the edge and the centre comes out clean. Allow to stand for 5–10 minutes to set completely before serving.
7. Serve the quiche, warm or cold, cut into wedges with a crisp salad.

FREEZING DETAILS
1. Prepare the recipe to the end of Step 6.
2. Cool quickly, pack in a rigid container, cover, seal, label and freeze for up to 2 months.

REHEATING DETAILS
Power setting: Full/Maximum
Defrosting and cooking time: 9–10 minutes
1. Remove all wrappings. Cook for 4–5 minutes, turning once. Allow to stand for 3 minutes to serve cold.
2. Cook for a further 2 minutes to reheat to serve warm.

COMBINATION OVENS:
Prepare and cook as above to the end of Step 3. Use the pastry to line a 20 cm (8 inch) flan dish or tin (if your make of oven recommends this). Ignore Step 4. Proceed from Step 5 using *microwave only* but increase the cooking time to 2½–3½ minutes. Place the courgettes in the quiche with the tomatoes and cheese. Pour over the uncooked milk mixture and *combination bake* at 200°C using *low* power for 20–25 minutes.
Reheating details: Follow the instructions above using *microwave only* but increase the cooking times in Step 1 to 4½–5¾ minutes and in Step 2 to 2–2½ minutes.

RIGHT: Tomato and courgette quiche

STUFFED AUBERGINES

2 x 225 g (8 oz) aubergines
1 tablespoon oil
1 large onion, peeled and chopped
2 large tomatoes, peeled, seeded and
  chopped
50 g (2 oz) cooked brown rice
50 g (2 oz) Feta cheese, crumbled
50 g (2 oz) chopped nuts, e.g. peanuts or
  cashews
2 tablespoons chopped fresh parsley
salt
freshly ground black pepper
4 tablespoons grated Parmesan cheese
  (optional)
sprigs of parsley, to garnish

Power setting: Full/Maximum
Preparation and cooking time: 20–25
minutes

1. Peel the stalks from the aubergines. Rinse and dry the aubergines and brush with a little of the oil. Place on a paper towel and cook for 4–6 minutes, turning over once. Leave to stand for 5 minutes, then cut in half lengthways and scoop out the flesh, keeping the skins intact.
2. Place the remaining oil in a bowl with the onion. Cover and cook for 3 minutes, stirring once.
3. Add the tomatoes, rice and chopped aubergine flesh, blending well. Cover and cook for 4 minutes, stirring once.
4. Add the Feta cheese, nuts, parsley and salt and pepper to taste, blending well. Spoon equally into the aubergine cases and place in a shallow cooking dish. Sprinkle with the Parmesan cheese, if using. Cover and cook for 2–3 minutes until hot.

5. Garnish with parsley sprigs and serve hot with a crisp salad.

COMBINATION OVENS:
Prepare and cook as above using *microwave only* but increase the cooking times in Step 1 to 4½–7 minutes; step 2 to 3½ minutes; Step 3 to 4½–5 minutes and Step 4 to 2½–3½ minutes.

VEGETABLE LASAGNE

1 onion, peeled and sliced
225 g (8 oz) carrots, peeled and sliced
2 leeks, scrubbed, trimmed and chopped
1 parsnip, peeled and thinly sliced
2 baby turnips, peeled and finely chopped
3 tablespoons water
50 g (2 oz) butter
50 g (2 oz) flour
600 ml (1 pint) milk
100 g (4 oz) Cheddar cheese, grated
salt
freshly ground black pepper
2 tomatoes, chopped
175 g (6 oz) no-need-to-precook lasagne
2 tablespoons dry breadcrumbs
2 tablespoons grated Parmesan cheese

Power setting: Full/Maximum and
Medium
Preparation and cooking time: about
30–35 minutes

1. Place the onion, carrots, leeks, parsnip and turnips in a bowl with the water. Cover and cook on full/maximum power for 10–12 minutes, until tender, stirring twice. Drain thoroughly.
2. Place the butter in a bowl and cook on full/maximum power for 1½ minutes to melt. Stir in the flour, then blend in the milk. Cook on full/maximum power for 6 minutes, stirring every minute until smooth, boiling and thickened. Stir in the cheese and salt and pepper to taste.
3. Mix the tomatoes with the cooked vegetables. Layer the lasagne with the cheese sauce and vegetables in a greased 23 cm (9 inch) square dish, finishing with a layer of sauce.
4. Sprinkle with the breadcrumbs and cheese and cook on full/maximum power for 9 minutes. Reduce the power level to medium and cook for a further 3–5

minutes until cooked through, hot and bubbly. Brown under a preheated hot grill if liked.

COMBINATION OVENS:
Prepare and cook as above using *microwave only* to the end of Step 3 but increase the cooking times in Step 1 on full/maximum power to 11½–14 minutes and Step 2 on full/maximum power to 1½–2 minutes then 7 minutes. Sprinkle with the breadcrumbs and cheese and *combination bake* at 200°C using *medium* power for 20 minutes.

FROM THE LEFT: Stuffed aubergines; Vegetable lasagne

MEAT

Whatever the occasion, from a ritual family gathering at Sunday lunch, a spur of the moment picnic with friends to a supper tray in front of the television or a mid-week dinner for special guests, the microwave will ensure that your meat dish is cooked succulently and speedily and with little attention. Generally speaking, cook the meat first, then leave it to stand, covered with foil, while cooking any accompaniments.

Steak sizzlers (recipe, page 40)

CASSOULET

350 g (12 oz) bacon pieces or forehock, cut
  into bite-sized pieces
175 g (6 oz) garlic sausage, cut into bite-
  sized pieces
1 x 425 g (15 oz) can red kidney beans,
  drained
1 x 425 g (15 oz) can butterbeans, drained
1 x 400 g (14 oz) can peeled tomatoes
2 onions, peeled and sliced
100 ml (4 fl oz) vegetable stock
freshly ground black pepper
1 tablespoon cornflour
120 g (4 oz) breadcrumbs (optional)
chopped fresh parsley, to garnish

Power setting: Full/Maximum
Preparation and cooking time: 30
minutes

1. Place the bacon, garlic sausage, kidney beans, butterbeans, tomatoes, onions, stock and pepper to taste in a large casserole and stir to mix. Cover and cook on full/maximum power for 10 minutes, stirring once.
2. Reduce the power setting to medium and cook for a further 15 minutes, stirring twice.
3. Mix the cornflour with a little water and stir into the cassoulet, blending well. Cook at full/maximum power for 3 minutes, stirring every 1 minute until thickened.
4. Sprinkle with the breadcrumbs, if using, and cook under a preheated hot grill until golden. Serve hot, straight from the dish, garnished with chopped parsley.

COMBINATION OVENS:
Prepare and cook as above using *microwave only* to the end of Step 1 but increase the cooking time in Step 1 to 11½ minutes. Stir in the cornflour, blending well and sprinkle with the breadcrumbs. *Combination bake* at 180°C using *low* power for 40 minutes, until browned and crisp, and the vegetables and meat are tender. Serve hot, straight from the dish.

BEEF AND WALNUT CASSEROLE

750 g (1½ lb) good quality braising or
  frying steak, cubed
1 tablespoon oil
1 garlic clove, peeled and crushed
300 ml (½ pint) beef stock or red wine
2 teaspoons Meaux mustard
pinch of dried tarragon
pinch of dried marjoram
1 tablespoon dry sherry (optional)
salt
freshly ground black pepper
100 g (4 oz) walnut pieces
1 tablespoon plain flour
water to mix

To garnish:
plain unsweetened yogurt
sprigs of watercress

Power setting: Full/Maximum
Preparation and cooking time: 35–40
minutes, plus standing

1. Place the steak, oil and garlic in a medium casserole. Cover and cook for 10 minutes, stirring once.
2. Add the stock or wine, mustard, tarragon, marjoram, sherry, if using, and salt and pepper to taste, blending well. Cover and cook for 10 minutes, stirring once.
3. Add the walnut pieces and the flour, mixed with a little cold water, and stir well to blend. Cover and cook for 5 minutes, stirring twice.
4. Leave to stand, covered, for 10–15 minutes, then spoon on to individual plates and make a swirl of plain yogurt over each one. Garnish with sprigs of watercress and serve with noodles and a green salad.

COMBINATION OVENS:
Brown the meat conventionally in a frying pan, if liked. Place all the ingredients except the walnuts and flour in a medium caserole, adding 120 ml (4 fl oz) extra hot beef stock or red wine. Cover and *combination bake* at 170°C using *low* power for 1 hour 10 minutes until tender, stirring halfway through the cooking time. Stir in the walnuts and the flour mixture about 10 minutes before the end of the cooking time. Garnish as above. A less prime cut of meat could be used for this method of cooking – like shin or skirt of beef, for example.

FROM THE TOP: Cassoulet; Beef and walnut casserole

BEEF AND ORANGE CASSEROLE

750 g (1½ lb) good quality braising or
  frying steak, cubed
1 tablespoon oil
1 onion, peeled and chopped
1 garlic clove, peeled and crushed
120 ml (4 fl oz) hot beef stock
120 ml (4 fl oz) orange juice
pinch of dried thyme
pinch of dried marjoram
1 bay leaf
salt
freshly ground black pepper
175 g (6 oz) button mushrooms
2 tablespoons cornflour
water, to mix

To garnish:
chopped fresh parsley
strips of orange rind

Power setting: Full/Maximum
Preparation and cooking time: 45–30
minutes, plus standing

1. Place the steak, oil, onion and garlic in a medium casserole. Cover and cook for 10 minutes, stirring once.
2. Add the stock, orange juice, thyme, marjoram, bay leaf and salt and pepper to taste, blending well. Cover and cook for 10 minutes, stirring once.
3. Add the mushrooms and the cornflour mixed with a little cold water and stir well to blend. Cover and cook for 5 minutes, stirring twice.
4. Leave to stand, covered, for 10–15 minutes before removing the bay leaf and serving garnished with the chopped parsley or strips of orange rind.

COMBINATION OVENS:
Brown the meat conventionally in a frying pan, if liked. Place all the ingredients except the cornflour in a medium casserole and add 150 ml (¼ pint) extra beef stock. Cover and *combination bake* at 170°C using *low* power for 1 hour 10 minutes until ten-

der, stirring halfway through the cooking time. Add the cornflour mixed with a little water about 10 minutes before the end of the cooking time. A less prime cut of meat could be used for this method of cooking – shin or skirt of beef, for example.

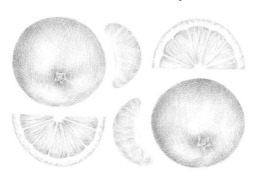

STEAK SIZZLERS

4 x 100 g (4 oz) minute steaks, beaten very
  thin
1 tablespoon crushed black peppercorns
salt
25 g (1 oz) butter
4 large slices toast, lightly buttered
2 tablespoons brandy, Madeira or rich beef
  stock
120 ml (4 fl oz) double cream
sprigs of parsley, to garnish

Power setting: Full/Maximum
Preparation and cooking time: about 15
minutes

1. Lightly coat both sides of each steak with peppercorns and season with salt.
2. Preheat a browning dish for 5 minutes on full/maximum power (or according to the manufacturer's handbook).
3. Add the butter and cook for 30 seconds. Place the steaks in the browning dish, pressing them down well, and cook for 5–6 minutes until they are cooked, turning them over after 2 minutes.
4. Remove the steaks and place each one on a piece of warm buttered toast.
5. Add the brandy to the juices in the browning dish, blending well. Stir in the cream and cook for 1–2 minutes until the sauce is bubbly and thick, stirring once. Spoon over the steaks, garnish, and serve at once.

COMBINATION OVENS:
If your oven does not have a grill facility, prepare and cook as above, using a browning dish and *microwave only* but increase the cooking times in Step 3 to 30–45 seconds, then 6–7 minutes and Step 5 to 1¼–2¼ minutes. If your oven has a grill facility, butter the steaks and place on the high grill rack. Cook under a hot grill for 3–5 minutes, turning over once. Prepare the sauce as above using the meat juices and cooking on *microwave only* as in Step 5.

FROM THE TOP: Beef and orange casserole; Steak sizzlers

GAMMON STEAKS WITH ORANGE AND HONEY

4 x 100 g (4 oz) gammon or bacon steaks
grated rind and juice of 1 orange
2 tablespoons thick honey
2 tablespoons soy sauce
pinch of dried sage

To garnish:
4 orange twists
sprigs of fresh sage

Power setting: Full/Maximum
Preparation and cooking time: 10
minutes

1. Remove the rind, then snip off the fat from the gammon or bacon steaks, if necessary. Place the steaks in a large shallow dish.
2. Mix the orange juice with the honey, soy sauce and sage, blending well. Pour the mixture over the steaks, cover and cook for 4 minutes, rearranging once. Leave to stand, covered, for 5 minutes.
3. Serve the gammon or bacon steaks coated with the orange and honey sauce and garnish each one with a single orange twist and a sprig of sage.

COMBINATION OVENS:
Prepare and cook as above using *microwave only* but increase the cooking time in Step 2 to 4¾–5 minutes.

BEEF AND KIDNEY HORSERADISH STEW

450 g (1 lb) good quality braising or frying
steak, cut into 2.5 cm (1 inch) pieces
175 g (6 oz) beef kidney, skinned, cored and
diced
1 tablespoon oil
2 onions, peeled and cut into eighths
175 g (6 oz) carrots, peeled and thinly
sliced
3 celery sticks, scrubbed and sliced
300 ml (½ pint) hot beef stock
2 tablespoons horseradish mustard
2 teaspoons soy sauce
salt
freshly ground black pepper
1 tablespoon flour
water to mix
bay leaves, to garnish

Croûtons:
25 g (1 oz) butter
6–8 thin slices French bread, cubed or left
whole

Power setting: Full/Maximum
Preparation and cooking time: about
50 minutes

1. Place the beef, kidney, oil, onions, carrots and celery in a casserole dish. Cover and cook for 15 minutes, stirring once.
2. Add the stock, mustard and soy sauce to the casserole. Season with salt and pepper and blend well. Cover and cook for a further 15 minutes, stirring once.
3. Mix the flour with a little water and stir it into the stew, blending well. Cover and cook for 5 minutes, stirring twice. Leave to stand, covered, for 10 minutes.
4. To make the croûtons, place the butter in a large shallow dish and cook for 30 seconds. Add the French bread and toss to coat. Cook for 2–3 minutes until the croûtons are crisp and brown, turning them over and rearranging them every 1 minute.
5. Serve the stew hot, topped with the crispy French bread croûtons and garnished with bay leaves.

COMBINATION OVENS:
Brown the meat conventionally in a frying pan, if liked. Place all the ingredients except the flour, bay leaves and croûton ingredients in a medium casserole, adding 150 ml (¼ pint) extra beef stock. Cover and *combination bake* at 170° C using *low* power for 1 hour 10 minutes until tender, stirring halfway through the cooking time. Stir in the flour mixture about 10 minutes before the end of the cooking time. Prepare the croûtons as in Step 4 above using *microwave only* but increase the cooking time to 2½–3½ minutes.

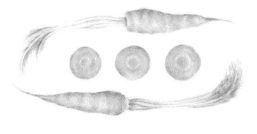

FROM THE TOP: Gammon steaks with orange and honey; Beef and kidney horseradish stew

RACK OF LAMB WITH WALNUT STUFFING

2 best ends of lamb, about 6–7 cutlets each
2 tablespoons orange jelly marmalade

Stuffing:
15 g (½ oz) butter
1 small onion, peeled and chopped
50 g (2 oz) fresh breadcrumbs
grated rind of ½ orange
chopped flesh of ½ orange
1 tablespoon chopped fresh parsley
25 g (1 oz) walnuts, chopped
75 g (3 oz) mellow Danish blue cheese,
  crumbled
salt
freshly ground black pepper
2 tablespoons beaten egg

To garnish:
cutlet frills
cherry tomatoes

Power setting: Full/Maximum and
Medium High
Preparation and cooking time: about
45 minutes, plus standing

1. Place the butter and onion in a bowl.
Cover and cook on full/maximum power
for 2 minutes, stirring once.
2. Add the breadcrumbs, orange rind,
orange flesh, parsley, walnuts, cheese and
salt and pepper to taste, blending well.
Bind together with the beaten egg.
3. Trim away any fat from the top 4 cm
(1½ inches) of the cutlet bones. Score dia-
gonally through the fat and stand the best
ends upright with the bone sides facing
and interweave the bone tips to make a
guard of honour shape. Tie the joints together at each end with thin string and fill
the cavity with the stuffing.
4. Stand the joint on a roasting rack in a
dish. Brush with the marmalade and cook
at medium high power for 20 minutes,
turning the dish once.
5. Brush again with a little oil and cook at
medium high power for a further 15
minutes, turning the dish once. Cover
with foil and leave to stand for 10–15
minutes.
6. Transfer to a warmed serving dish and

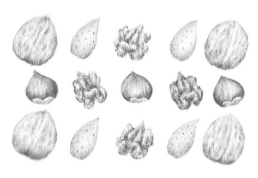

garnish the bone tips with the cutlet frills
and cherry tomatoes. Serve the new
potatoes and green vegetables.

COMBINATION OVENS:
Prepare and cook as above using *microwave only* to the end of Step 3 but increase
the cooking time in Step 1 to 2½ minutes.
Brush the outside of the prepared roast
with oil and place in a shallow dish. *Combination bake* at 200°C using *low* power for
50 minutes. Garnish as above.

CHILLI LAMB FIESTA

4 large lamb loin chops, about 175 g (6 oz)
  each, trimmed of excess fat
25 g (1 oz) butter
½ small onion, peeled and chopped
½ green pepper, cored, seeded and chopped
½ red pepper, cored, seeded and chopped
1 carrot, peeled and sliced
175 g (6 oz) baby sweetcorns or sweetcorn
  kernels
1 x 425 g (15 oz) can chilli beans
sprigs of rosemary, to garnish

Power setting: Full/Maximum
Preparation and cooking time: 25
minutes

1. Preheat a large browning dish on full/
maximum power for 5 minutes (or according to the manufacturer's instructions).
Add the lamb chops so that the meatiest
portions are to the outer edge of the dish.
Cook for 8–9 minutes, turning over once.
Leave to stand, covered, while preparing
the vegetable mixture.
2. Place the butter, onion, green and red
peppers, carrot and sweetcorn in a large
shallow dish. Cover and cook for 6
minutes, stirring twice.
3. Add the chilli beans, blending well.
Cover and cook for 2 minutes, stirring
once.
4. Add the chops to the bean mixture and

coat lightly with a little of the juices. Cover
and cook for 1–2 minutes until hot. Garnish with sprigs of rosemary and serve.

COMBINATION OVENS:
Place the chops in a shallow dish and *combination bake* at 250°C using *medium*
for 12–15 minutes, turning over once.
Continue as above from Step 2 using
microwave only but increase the cooking
times in Step 2 to 7 minutes; Step 3 to 2½
minutes and Step 4 to 1¼–2½ minutes.

*FROM THE TOP: Rack of lamb with walnut stuff-
ing; Chilli lamb fiesta*

RICE–STUFFED BREAST OF LAMB

25 g (1 oz) butter
350 g (12 oz) cooked long-grain rice
50 g (2 oz) raisins
grated rind and juice of 1 orange
25 g (1 oz) walnuts, chopped
salt
freshly ground black pepper
1 egg, beaten
1 breast of lamb, boned
1 garlic clove, peeled and cut into slivers
sprigs of rosemary, to garnish

Power setting: Full/Maximum
Preparation and cooking time: about
40 minutes

1. Place the butter in a bowl and cook for 1 minute. Add the rice, raisins, orange rind and juice, walnuts and salt and pepper to taste, blending well. Bind together with the beaten egg.
2. Lay the breast of lamb flat, skin side down, on a board and spread the stuffing over the flesh, reserving any extra. Roll up and secure neatly with string. Make deep incisions into the meat with a sharp knife and insert the garlic slivers.
3. Place on a roasting rack in a shallow dish, cover and cook for 28 minutes, giving the dish a quarter–turn every 7 minutes.
4. Spoon any reserved rice mixture on to a serving dish and top with the stuffed breast of lamb. Cook for a further 2 minutes to serve. Brown under a pre-heated hot grill to crisp, if liked, before garnishing and serving.

COMBINATION OVENS:
Prepare and cook as above using *microwave only* to the end of Step 2 but increase the cooking time in Step 1 to 1¼ minutes. Weigh the stuffed joint and *combination bake* at 220°C using *medium* power for 13–14 minutes per 450 g (1 lb), turning over halfway through the cooking time and basting regularly. Leave to stand for 10 minutes before serving. Continue from Step 4 using *microwave only* and increasing the cooking time to 2½ minutes.

LAMB AND POTATO BRAISE

6 middle neck lamb chops
1 kg (2 lb) potatoes, peeled and diced
1 large onion, peeled and chopped
1 x 400 g (14 oz) can chopped tomatoes
¼ teaspoon dried oregano
¼ teaspoon dried thyme
¼ teaspoon dried rosemary
salt
freshly ground black pepper
2 tablespoons dry sherry
sprigs of thyme, to garnish

Power setting: Full/Maximum
Preparation and cooking time: about
45–50 minutes

1. Preheat a large browning dish for about 5 minutes (or according to the manufacturer's instructons). Add the lamb chops, ensuring that the meatiest portions are to the outer edge of the dish. Cook for 8 minutes, turning over once. Leave the chops to stand while preparing the vegetable mixture.
2. Place the potatoes, onion, tomatoes, oregano, thyme, rosemary and salt and pepper to taste in a large shallow casserole. Cover and cook for 20 minutes, stirring gently twice.
3. Arrange the chops on top of the vegetables, pour over the sherry, cover and cook for a further 2–3 minutes until the vegetables are tender and the meat is hot and fully cooked.
4. Garnish with sprigs of fresh thyme and serve hot with a green vegetable.

COMBINATION OVENS:
Place the chops in a shallow dish and *combination bake* at 250°C using *medium* power for 12–15 minutes, turning over once until just cooked. Continue as above from Step 2 using *microwave only* but increase the cooking time in Step 2 to 23–24 minutes. Arrange the chops on top of the vegetables, pour over the sherry and cook, uncovered, on *combination bake* at 250°C using *medium* power for a further 5 minutes until hot and the vegetables are tender. Garnish as above to serve.

FROM THE LEFT: Rice-stuffed breast of lamb; Lamb and potato braise

ROAST VEAL WITH MANDARIN ORANGES

SERVES 6
1 x 1.5 kg (3½ lb) veal roast
½ teaspoon dried oregano
½ teaspoon dried basil
1 teaspoon ground paprika
salt
freshly ground black pepper
5 tablespoons dry white wine
sprigs of parsley, to garnish

Sauce:
150 ml (¼ pint) chicken stock
1 x 200 g (7 oz) can mandarin oranges in
   natural juice
2 teaspoons plain flour
3 tablespoons single cream
3 tablespoons dry white wine

Power setting: Medium and Full/
Maximum
Preparation and cooking time: about 1
hour, plus standing

1. Season the veal with the oregano, basil, paprika and salt and pepper to taste. Place in a shallow cooking dish with the wine. Cook on medium power for 18 minutes.
2. Turn the veal over and cook on medium power for 18–24 minutes, until tender. Remove from the dish with a slotted spoon. Wrap in foil, shiny side inside, and leave to stand for 20 minutes.
3. Meanwhile, stir the chicken stock and mandarin juice into the meat juices, blending well. Blend the flour with the cream to a smooth paste and stir into the sauce mixture with the wine, blending well. Cook on full/maximum power for 3–5 minutes, stirring three times, until smooth, boiling and thickened.
4. Stir in the mandarins and cook on full/maximum power for 1 minute.
5. Place the veal on a warmed serving plate, garnish, and serve with the hot mandarin sauce.

COMBINATION OVENS:
Season the veal with the oregano, basil, paprika and salt and pepper to taste. Place in a shallow cooking dish with the wine. *Comination bake* at 220° C using *low* power for 35–40 minutes, turning the joint over once. Remove from the dish with a slotted spoon and leave to stand for 10 minutes.

It is essential if using canned mandarins to use those in natural orange juice rather than in syrup for this recipe, otherwise the sauce will be too sweet. Should you wish to use fresh mandarins (or satsumas or tangerines), then you will need the segments from 4–5 mandarins and the juice from another 3–4.

HONEY AND PINEAPPLE PORK PARCELS

4 large pork loin chops, about 175–225 g
   (6–8 oz) each
1 x 225 g (8 oz) can pineapple slices in
   natural juice, drained and juice reserved
2 tablespoons clear honey
1 tablespoon soy sauce
1 tablespoon lemon juice
salt
freshly ground black pepper
sprigs of sage, to garnish

Power setting: Full/Maximum
Preparation and cooking time: 15–20
minutes, plus standing

1. Top each pork chop with a pineapple slice and place one in a small roasting bag.
2. Mix 2 tablespoons of the reserved pineapple juice with the honey, soy sauce, lemon juice and salt and pepper to taste, blending well. Spoon equally into the bags over the meat and secure the necks of the bags loosely with elastic bands or string.
3. Place the bags on a large plate and cook for 8–10 minutes, until cooked and tender, rearranging twice. Leave to stand for 5 minutes.
4. Remove from the bags and arrange on a warmed serving dish. Cook under a preheated hot grill until golden, if liked. Garnish with sprigs of sage and serve immediately with mashed potatoes and a green vegetable.

COMBINATION OVENS:
Prepare and cook as above using *microwave only* but increase the cooking times in Step 3 to 9½–11½ minutes.

FROM THE LEFT: Roast veal with mandarin oranges; Honey and pineapple pork parcels

PICNIC LOIN OF PORK WITH MILD MUSTARD SAUCE

SERVES 6–8

1 x 1 kg (2 lb) boned and rolled loin of pork,
* rind removed*
10–12 stoned prunes
salt
freshly ground black pepper
100 ml (3½ fl oz) hot chicken or light meat
* stock*
3 tablespoons made mild mustard
2 tablespoons dry white wine
150 ml (¼ pint) thick set natural yogurt

Power setting: Full/Maximum
Preparation and cooking time: about
25–30 minutes, plus cooling

1. Using a sharp knife, make an incision through the centre of the joint and press in the prunes. Season with salt and pepper to taste and place in a roasting dish.
2. Mix the stock with the mustard, pour over the pork, cover and cook for 16–20 minutes until the pork is tender, turning over and rearranging twice. Leave to stand, covered, until cold, then remove the meat from the juices.
3. Skim off any fat from the pan juices and add the wine. Cook, uncovered, for 3 minutes. Leave to cool.
4. When the juices have cooled completely, blend them with the yogurt and season to taste with the salt and pepper.
5. Cut the meat into slices and serve it with the cold mustard sauce, a crisp salad garnish and some crusty wholemeal bread.

COMBINATION OVENS:
Prepare and cook as above using *microwave only* but increase the cooking times in Step 2 to 18½–23½ minutes and Step 3 to 3½ minutes.

Many microwave cooks prefer to pre-brown their roasts, hotpots and meat dishes to give a traditional or oven-baked appearance. Until recently browning dishes and skillets were the only way to brown food efficiently in the microwave; now there are special microwave browning casseroles too. Coated with the same base as other browning dishes, they make pre-browning of meat for larger casserole mixtures ultra convenient. There is no need to pre-brown combination oven dishes; they will brown naturally because of the use of microwave and convection heat.

STIR–FRIED LIVER

450 g (1 lb) lamb's liver, cut into strips
2 tablespoons orange juice
1 tablespoon dry sherry
2.5 cm (1 inch) piece fresh root ginger,
* peeled and finely chopped*
25 g (1 oz) butter
8 spring onions, trimmed and cut into 5 cm
* (2 inch) pieces*
1 small red pepper, cored, seeded and sliced
* into strips*
1 carrot, peeled and coarsely grated
1 x 425 g (15 oz) can Calypso beans (or
* 300 ml (½ pint) cooked haricot beans in a*
* sweet and sour sauce)*

Power setting: Full/Maximum
Preparation and cooking time: 10–15
minutes, plus marinating

1. Place the liver, orange juice, sherry and ginger in a bowl. Cover and leave to marinate for 30 minutes. Drain the liver and reserve the marinade.
2. Place the butter in a large dish and cook for 1 minute to melt. Add the drained liver, spring onions, red pepper and carrot and cook for 7–8 minutes, stirring twice, or until the lamb is just tender and the vegetables are softened but still crisp.
3. Add the beans and the reserved marinade, blending well. Cover and cook for 3 minutes, stirring once, until hot and bubbly. Serve at once.

COMBINATION OVENS:
Prepare and cook as above using *microwave only* but increase the cooking times in Step 2 to 1¼ minutes then 8–9½ minutes and Step 3 to 3½ minutes.

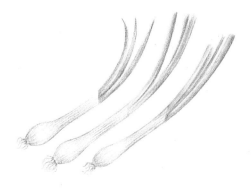

FROM THE TOP: Picnic loin of pork with mild mustard sauce; Stir-fried liver

CARIBBEAN PORK

350 g (12 oz) boneless pork, sliced into thin
  strips
½ red pepper, cored, seeded and sliced
½ green pepper, cored, seeded and sliced
6 spring onions, trimmed and sliced
1 x 375 g (13 oz) can crushed pineapple
1 tablespoon soy sauce
1 teaspoon Angostura bitters
1 tablespoon tomato ketchup
175 g (6 oz) long-grain rice
600 ml (1 pint) boiling water
salt
freshly ground black pepper

Power setting: Full/Maximum
Preparation and cooking time: about
25 minutes, plus standing

1. Place the pork, red and green peppers
and spring onions in a large casserole.
Cover and cook for 7 minutes, stirring
once.
2. Add the pineapple and its juice, the soy
sauce, Angostura bitters, tomato ketchup,
rice, boiling water and salt and pepper to
taste, blending well. Cover and cook for
13–15 minutes, stirring twice, until the rice
is just tender and the liquid is absorbed.
3. Leave to stand, covered, for 10 minutes.
Fluff up the mixture with a fork and serve
immediately.

COMBINATION OVENS:
Prepare and cook as above using *microwave only* but increase the cooking times in
Step 1 to 7¼ minutes and Step 2 to 15–17½
minutes.

SAUSAGE BRIOCHES

4 large spicy sausages
15 g (½ oz) butter
50 g (2 oz) button mushrooms, wiped and
  sliced
1–2 teaspoons horseradish or ready-made
  mustard
4 tablespoons mayonnaise, double cream,
  soured cream or set plain unsweetened
  yogurt
salt
freshly ground black pepper
2 teaspoons chopped fresh parsley
4 baker's individual unsweeted brioches or 1
  large unsweetened brioche

Power setting: Full/Maximum
Preparation and cooking time: about
10–15 minutes

1. Prick the sausages and place them on a
roasting rack over a dish or on a large
plate. Leave to stand for 3 minutes, then
cut into bite-sized pieces.
2. Place the butter in a bowl with the
mushrooms. Cover and cook for 1–1½
minutes, until tender.
3. Drain the mushrooms and mix them
with the sausage pieces. Add the mustard,
mayonnaise, cream or yogurt and salt and
pepper to taste, blending well.
4. Remove the 'caps' from the brioches,
scoop out and discard the soft bread inside
(or reserve it to use for another dish) and
spoon in the sausage mixture. Sprinkle
with the parsley.
5. Replace the caps and stand the brioches
on a double thickness sheet of absorbent
paper towels. Cook for 1–1½ minutes until
they are just hot – take care not to overcook or the brioches will become soggy.
6. Serve at once with a salad. If you have

used a large brioche, then cut into 4 thick
wedges to serve.

COMBINATION OVENS:
Prepare and cook as above using *microwave only* to the end of Step 4 but increase
the cooking times in Step 1 to 4½ minutes
and Step 2 to 1¼–1¾ minutes. Replace the
caps and stand the brioches in a shallow
ovenproof dish and *combination bake* at
250°C using *defrost* power for 3–5 minutes
until just hot.

*FROM THE LEFT: Caribbean pork; Sausage
brioches*

POULTRY AND GAME

Whether you opt to cook a huge turkey for a crowd, a tender young poussin for a single serving or perhaps a duck or a pheasant for two or three, the microwave will ensure that it is ready in next to no time. Larger birds will brown readily during their longer cooking times but portions and pieces may need the help of a browning agent, browning dish or hot conventional grill before, during or after cooking.

Chicken breasts in creamy summer sauce (recipe, page 58)

RABBIT HOTPOT WITH CARAWAY DUMPLINGS

1 onion, peeled and sliced into rings
1 garlic clove, peeled and crushed
4 rashers back bacon, rinded and chopped
25 g (1 oz) plain flour
200 ml (7 fl oz) dry cider
750 g (1½ lb) boneless rabbit, skinned and
*   cubed*
225 g (8 oz) button mushrooms, wiped and
*   sliced*
1 tablespoon chopped fresh parsley
1 small bay leaf
salt
freshly ground black pepper

Dumplings:
50 g (2 oz) butter or margarine
2 tablespoons parsley and thyme stuffing
*   mix*
¼ teaspoon caraway seeds
100 g (4 oz) plain flour
1 heaped teaspoon baking power
4 tablespoons cold water

Power setting: Full/Maximum
Preparation and cooking time: about
45 minutes

1. Place the onion rings and crushed garlic in a small bowl. Cover the bowl and cook for 2–3 minutes, then remove and set aside.

2. Place the bacon in a large casserole dish. Cook for 4 minutes until crisp, stirring twice. Using a slotted spoon, remove the bacon from the casserole dish.

3. Add the flour to the bacon fat, blending well. Gradually add the cider and blend thoroughly.

4. Add the rabbit, mushrooms, parsley, bacon, onion mixture, bay leaf and salt and pepper to taste, blending well. Cover and cook for 20–25 minutes or until the rabbit is cooked and tender, stirring 3 times.

5. To make the dumplings, place 25 g (1 oz) of the butter in a bowl and cook for 30 seconds to melt. Stir in the stuffing mix and caraway seeds.

6. Sift the flour into a mixing bowl with the baking powder and a pinch of salt. Rub in the remaining butter and mix with the water to a firm but pliable dough. Divide and shape into 8 balls, brush with a little water and roll in the stuffing mix. Arrange in a circle on top of the hotpot and cook for 8–10 minutes until the dumplings are well-risen, fluffy and cooked through. Serve at once with the hotpot.

COMBINATION OVENS:
Prepare and cook as above using *microwave only* to the end of Step 3 but increase the cooking times in Step 1 to 2½–3½ minutes and Step 2 to 4¾ minutes. Add the rabbit, mushrooms, parsley, bacon, onion mixture, bay leaf and salt and pepper to taste, blending well. Cover and *combination bake* at 200°C using *low* power for 20 minutes. Prepare the dumplings as in Steps 5 and 6 above. Add to the casserole, basting well with the stock. Cover and *combination bake* at 200°C using *low* power for 10 minutes. Remove the lid and cook by *convection only* at 200°C for a further 10 minutes. Serve at once.

Hotpots, casseroles and slow-cooked stews are favourite winter warmers that respond well to cooking in the combination microwave. If you have a favourite chicken or rabbit recipe that you would like to cook this way, then, as a general rule, cook it on a slightly higher temperature than usual, say 200°C and use Low power for about 25–35 minutes, depending upon size and tenderness of the poultry pieces.

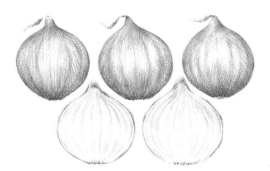

RIGHT: Rabbit hotpot with caraway dumplings

CHICKEN BREASTS IN CREAMY SUMMER SAUCE

4 chicken breasts, about 225 g (8 oz) each,
  skinned
1 x 295 g (10 oz) can condensed cream of
  asparagus soup
100 g (4 oz) mushrooms, wiped and sliced
5 tablespoons dry white wine
2 tablespoons chopped fresh parsley
salt
freshly ground black pepper
sprigs of watercress, to garnish

Power setting: Full/Maximum and
Medium
Preparation and cooking time: 25
minutes, plus standing

1. Place the chicken breasts in a shallow dish. Add the soup, mushrooms, wine, parsley and salt and pepper to taste.
2. Cover and cook on full/maximum power for 5 minutes.
3. Stir well to blend and rearrange the chicken. Cover and cook on medium power for 15 minutes, stirring once.
4. Leave to stand, covered, for 5 minutes before serving, garnished with watercress sprigs.

COMBINATION OVENS:
Prepare and cook as above using *microwave only* but increase the cooking times in Step 2 on full/maximum power to 6 minutes and Step 3 on medium power to 17½ minutes.

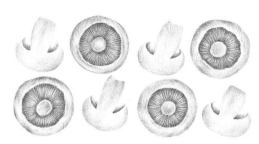

MUSTARD CHICKEN CASSEROLE

1 x 1.5 kg (3½ lb) roasting chicken, cut into
  8 pieces and skinned
8 rashers back bacon, rinded
1 teaspoon wholegrain mustard
1 teaspoon English mustard
2 tablespoons plain flour
350 ml (12 fl oz) hot chicken stock
dash of lemon juice
freshly ground black pepper
sprigs of parsley, to garnish

Power setting: Full/Maximum
Preparation and cooking time: about
35 minutes

1. Wrap each piece of chicken in a rasher of bacon and secure with a wooden cocktail stick. Prick with a fork and place in a serving dish with the boniest parts of the chicken towards the centre. Cover and cook for 10 minutes.
2. Remove the partially cooked chicken with a slotted spoon. Stir the mustards and the flour into the chicken juices and blend in well. Gradually add the hot chicken stock and the lemon juice, then cook for 2 minutes, stirring twice.
3. Return the chicken pieces to the dish, add pepper to taste and coat with the mustard flavoured stock. Cover and cook for 10–14 minutes, rearranging and turning over twice, until the chicken is just cooked. Leave to stand, covered, for 5–10 minutes, then remove the cocktail sticks and garnish with the sprigs of parsley.

COMBINATION OVENS:
Prepare and cook as above using *microwave only* to the end of Step 3, then *combination bake* at 220° C using *low* power for about 15 minutes or until the chicken is cooked, turning and rearranging the chicken twice.

FROM THE TOP: Chicken breasts in creamy summer sauce; Mustard chicken casserole

HONEY AND ORANGE POUSSINS

4 x 450 g (1 lb) poussins
3 tablespoons clear honey
1 teaspoon ground paprika
1 teaspoon soy sauce
150 ml (¼ pint) unsweetened orange juice
1 teaspoon finely grated orange rind
pinch of ground ginger
1 teaspoon cornflour
salt
freshly ground black pepper
sprigs of watercress, to garnish

Power setting: Full/Maximum
Preparation and cooking time: 40–45
minutes

1. Wash and dry the poussins. Mix the honey, paprika and soy sauce. Brush the poussins with half of the glaze and place them, breast downwards, on a roasting rack set in a dish. Cover loosely with greaseproof paper and cook for 20 minutes.
2. Rearrange the poussins so that the breast side is on top and brush with the remaining glaze. Cover and cook for 15-20 minutes, until tender. Leave to stand, covered, while making the sauce.
3. Drain the cooking juices into a jug. Add the orange juice, orange rind, ginger, cornflour and salt and pepper to taste, blending well. Cook for 2–3 minutes, stirring every 1 minute, until lightly thickened.
4. Pour a little of the sauce on to the serving dish and arrange the poussins over the top. Garnish, and serve hot with the remaining sauce separately.

COMBINATION OVENS:
Rinse and dry the poussins. Mix the honey, paprika, and soy sauce. Brush the poussins with half the glaze and place breast downwards, on a roasting rack set in a dish and *combination bake* at 220°C using *medium* power for 15 minutes. Rearrange the poussins so that the breast side is on top and brush with the remaining glaze. *Combination bake* at 220°C using *medium* power for 15 minutes. Leave to stand, covered, while making the sauce. Prepare it as in Steps 3 and 4 above using *microwave only* but increase the cooking time in Step 3 to 2½-3½ minutes.

CHICKEN BREASTS WITH BEAN SPROUTS AND WATER CHESTNUTS

350 g (12 oz) boneless chicken breasts,
  skinned and sliced into strips
1 carrot, peeled and sliced into julienne
  strips
100 g (4 oz) pak soi, bok choy cabbage or
  Savoy cabbage, finely shredded
6 spring onions, trimmed and sliced
100 g (4 oz) bean sprouts
100 g (4 oz) water chestnuts, sliced
150 ml (¼ pint) chicken stock
1 tablespoon soy sauce
1 tablespoon dry sherry
2 tablespoons cornflour
small pieces of fresh root ginger, peeled and
  grated
pinch of Chinese 5-spice powder
2 tablespoons toasted flaked almonds

Power setting: Full/Maximum
Preparation and cooking time: 15–20
minutes

1. Place the chicken, carrot and pak soi in a large bowl. Cover and cook for 6 minutes, stirring twice. Add the spring onions, bean sprouts and water chestnuts, blending well. Cover and cook for 1 minute.
2. Place the chicken stock, soy sauce, sherry, cornflour, grated ginger and 5–spice powder in another bowl, blending well. Cook for 2½–3 minutes, stirring every 1 minute until boiling, smooth and thickened.
3. Add the sauce to the chicken mixture and toss well to mix. Cook, uncovered, for 2–3 minutes until very hot, stirring once.
4. Serve immediately, sprinkled with toasted flaked almonds and accompanied by boiled rice.

COMBINATION OVENS:
Prepare and cook as above using *microwave only* but increase the cooking times in Step 1 to 7 minutes then, 1½ minutes; Step 2 to 3-3½ minutes and Step 3 to 2½-3½ minutes.

FROM THE LEFT: Chicken breasts with bean sprouts and water chestnuts; Honey and orange poussins

TURKEY AND BROCCOLI DIVAN

SERVES 6

75 g (3 oz) butter
2 tablespoons chopped fresh parsley
100 g (4 oz) fresh white breadcrumbs
225 g (8 oz) mushrooms, wiped and sliced
3 tablespoons plain flour
175 ml (6 fl oz) milk
150 ml (¼ pint) soured cream
salt
freshly ground black pepper
750 g (1½ lb) turkey fillets, thinly sliced
2 x 250 g (9 oz) packets frozen broccoli
  spears
grated Parmesan cheese (optional)

Power setting: Full/Maximum
Preparation and cooking time: about
45 minutes

1. Place 50 g (2 oz) of the butter in a bowl and cook for 30 seconds to melt. Add the parsley and breadcrumbs, blending well. Cook for 2–4 minutes, stirring frequently, until crisp and golden brown. Drain on absorbent paper towels.
2. Place the remaining butter in a bowl with the mushrooms and cook for 1 minute. Stir in the flour and the milk, blending well. Cook for 4 minutes, stirring every 1 minute until smooth and thickened. Blend in the soured cream and salt and pepper to taste.
3. Add the turkey fillet slices to the sauce, cover and cook for 13–15 minutes, stirring and rearranging twice.
4. Place the frozen broccoli spears in a bowl. Cover and cook for 2 minutes.

Separate the spears.
5. Place the broccoli in a single layer in the base of a heatproof serving dish. Spoon over the turkey mixture. Spoon the browned breadcrumbs around the edge of the dish and sprinkle with Parmesan cheese in the centre, if using. Cook, uncovered, for 5–8 minutes, until hot and bubbly, giving the dish a half–turn twice.
6. Serve hot with noodles or raisin rice.

COMBINATION OVENS:
Prepare and cook as above using *microwave only* but increase the cooking times in Step 1 to 40 seconds then 2½–4¾ minutes: Step 2 to 1¼ minutes then 4¾ minutes; Step 3 to 15–18½ minutes; Step 4 to 2½ minutes and Step 5 to 6–9 minutes.

MALAYSIAN CURRY

25 g (1 oz) creamed coconut, grated
75 ml (3 fl oz) hot water
750 g (1½ lb) boneless chicken breasts,
  skinned and cubed
450 g (1 lb) potatoes, peeled and cubed
2 tomatoes, quartered
1 x 425 g (15 oz) can medium curry cook-in
  sauce or 300 ml (½ pint) home-made well-
  flavoured curry sauce
1–2 tablespoons peanut butter
150 ml (¼ pint) single cream
50 g (2 oz) chopped peanuts
3 hard boiled eggs, shelled and quartered
sprigs of fresh coriander, to garnish

Power setting: Full/Maximum and
Medium
Preparation and cooking time: about
40 minutes

1. Place the grated coconut in a jug, pour on the hot water and stir until blended thoroughly.
2. Place the chicken, potatoes, tomatoes, curry sauce, coconut mixture, peanut butter, cream and peanuts in a casserole. Cover and cook on full/maximum power for 20 minutes, stirring twice.
3. Reduce the power setting and cook on medium power for 5–10 minutes or until the meat and vegetables are tender.
4. Stir in the hard-boiled eggs and serve hot, garnished with the coriander sprigs. Accompany with boiled rice, poppadums and a pickle or chutney.

COMBINATION OVENS:
Prepare and cook as above using *microwave only* but increase the cooking times in Step 2 on full/maximum power to 23½ minutes and Step 3 on medium power to 6–11½ minutes.

Coconut milk is used in curries from southern India and south-east Asia. It can be bought canned and ready to use, but can also be made from creamed or desiccated coconut. Blocks of creamed coconut should be simply grated and dissolved in a little hot water, according to the packet or recipe instructions. Desiccated coconut is cooked in hot water. Heat 50 g (2 oz) desiccated coconut with about 300 ml (½ pint) water until hot, then cover and leave to stand for 20 minutes. Strain to use.

*FROM THE LEFT: Turkey and broccoli divan;
Malaysian curry*

ROAST TURKEY WITH CRANBERRY STUFFING

SERVES 8
1 x 3.5 kg (8 lb) oven–ready turkey
25 g (1 oz) butter
sprigs of watercress, to garnish

Stuffing:
100 g (4 oz) fresh white breadcrumbs
175 g (6 oz) prunes, soaked overnight,
  stoned and chopped
2 dessert apples, peeled, cored and sliced
50 g (2 oz) blanched almonds, chopped
3 tablespoons cranberry sauce
grated rind and juice of 1 lemon
1 egg, beaten
salt
freshly ground black pepper

Power setting: Full/Maximum
Preparation and cooking time: about
1½ hours

1. To make the stuffing, mix the breadcrumbs with the prunes, apple, almonds, cranberry sauce, lemon rind, lemon juice, beaten egg and salt and pepper to taste, blending well. Use to stuff the neck end of the turkey, securing the opening with wooden cocktail sticks and truss the whole bird into an even shape.
2. Place the turkey, breast side down, in a large shallow dish and smear with the butter. Cook for 16 minutes.
3. Turn the bird on to one side and baste with the cooking juices. Cook for a further 16 minutes.
4. Turn the bird on to the second side and brush again to baste. Cook for a further 16 minutes.
5. At this stage, if some of the thinner and more vulnerable areas of the turkey begin to overcook then shield with small strips of foil but ensure that they do not touch the sides of the oven. Turn the turkey breast–side up and baste again. Cook for a further 16 minutes. Cover with foil and leave to stand for 15 minutes before serving, garnished with watercress sprigs.

COMBINATION OVENS:
Prepare as in Step 1 above then place in a shallow cooking dish and *combination bake* at 200°C using *medium* power for 54–63 minutes or at 220°C using *low* power for 72 minutes, turning twice and basting regularly during cooking. Leave to stand, covered with foil, for 15 minutes before serving.

DUCK WITH DAMSON SAUCE

1 x 2.25 kg (5 lb) oven–ready duckling,
  prepared for cooking
salt
freshly ground black pepper
1 x 450 g (1 lb) can damsons in syrup
25 g (1 oz) butter
1 onion, peeled and finely chopped
2 teaspoons soy sauce
½ teaspoon ground ginger

Power setting: Full/Maximum
Preparation and cooking time: about
50 minutes

FROM THE TOP: Roast turkey with cranberry stuffing; Duck with damson sauce

1. Remove any fat from inside the body of the duck. Secure any tail-end flaps of skin to the main body with wooden cocktail sticks. Shield the wing tips and legs with foil, as necessary, for half of the cooking time. Prick the skin thoroughly and season with salt and pepper. Place breast side down on a roasting rack set in a shallow dish and cook for 10 minutes.
2. Turn the duck over and drain away any excess fat. Cook for 15 minutes and drain again to remove excess fat.
3. Cook for a further 10–15 minutes until the duck when pierced yields clear, not pink, juices. Leave to stand, covered, while preparing the sauce. If liked, the duckling can now be crisped and browned under a preheated hot conventional grill.
4. To prepare the sauce, sieve the damsons and their juice to remove the stones. Place the butter in a bowl and cook for 30 seconds to melt. Add the onion and cook for 2 minutes. Stir in the damson purée, soy sauce and ground ginger. Cook, uncovered, for 5 minutes, stirring once.
5. Serve hot with the damson sauce.

COMBINATION OVENS:
Prepare the duckling as above and place on a roasting rack set in a shallow dish. *Combination bake* at 220°C using *low* power for 40–50 minutes, turning over twice and regularly removing any excess fat. Leave to stand, covered with foil, while preparing the sauce. Prepare the sauce as in Steps 4 and 5 above but increase the cooking times in Step 4 to 40 seconds, then 2½ minutes and then to 6 minutes.

TURKEY WITH YELLOW BEAN SAUCE

2 tablespoons sesame oil
450 g (1 lb) turkey breast, skinned and cut
 into strips
1 tablespoon grated fresh root ginger
4 tablespoons yellow bean stir-fry sauce
50 g (2 oz) roasted cashew nuts (optional)
100 g (4 oz) mangetout, trimmed
100 g (4 oz) canned whole baby sweetcorn
 in brine, drained or 100 g (4 oz) fresh
 baby sweetcorn, cooked

Power setting: Full/Maximum
Preparation and cooking time: 10–15
minutes

1. Place the oil in a bowl and cook for 1
minute until hot.
2. Add the turkey and ginger and blend
well, then cook for 3–4 minutes, stirring
every 1 minute.
3. Add the yellow bean sauce, cashew
nuts, if wished, mangetout and baby
sweetcorn, blending well. Cook for 3
minutes, stirring twice.
4. Serve at once with plain boiled rice.

COMBINATION OVENS:
Prepare and cook as above using *microwave only* but increase the cooking times in
Step 1 to 1¼ minutes; Step 2 to 3½–3¾
minutes and Step 3 to 3½ minutes.

PEKING DUCK

4 x 175 g (6 oz) duck fillets
soy sauce
120 ml (4 fl oz) hoi sin or plum sauce
 about 30–32 paper thin 15 cm (6 inch)
 conventionally-made pancakes made from
 600 ml (1 pint) milk, 2 eggs and 225 g
 (8 oz) plain flour
1 bunch spring onions, trimmed and sliced
 lengthways into thin pieces
15 cm (6 in) piece of cucumber, thinly sliced
 lengthways

Power setting: Medium High and Full/
Maximum
Preparation and cooking time: about
30 minutes, excluding pancakes

*FROM THE LEFT: Turkey with yellow bean sauce;
Peking duck*

The pancakes must be made in a frying
pan on a conventional hob. As they freeze
well, you can make a batch in advance and
keep them in the freezer for up to 4
months. They should be interleaved with
greaseproof paper and overwrapped with
foil. To use, unwrap the package and thaw
the pancakes at room temperature for
about 20 minutes. If you live near a
Chinese supermarket, you can save time
by buying ready-made frozen pancakes.
1. Make deep diagonal cuts into the skin of
the duck fillets and place them, skin side
up, on a roasting rack set over a dish.
Glaze with a little soy sauce, cover and
cook on medium high power for 15–20
minutes, turning and rearranging twice.
Crisp the skin under a preheated hot conventional grill, if liked, then slice the fillets
into thin slices.
2. Place the hoi sin or plum sauce in a bowl
and cook at full/maximum power for 2
minutes until it is hot.
3. Stack the pancakes on a plate and cover
them with a damp paper towel. Cook at
full/maximum power for 2 minutes until
they are just warmed through.
4. Serve the pancakes with the crispy duck,
the sauce, the spring onions and cucumber. To eat, place a little of the sauce on
each pancake, top with a little of the duck,
some spring onions and cucumber. Roll
up the pancakes and eat with your fingers.

COMBINATION OVENS:
Prepare and cook as above using *microwave only* but increase the cooking times in
Step 1 on medium power to 24–36 minutes; Step 2 on full/maximum power to 2½
minutes and Step 3 on full/maximum
power for 2¼–2½ minutes. If your microwave has a grill facility the duck fillets may
be cooked on the grill rack on *grill high* for
10–12 minutes, turning over twice until
crisp, brown and cooked through.

PHEASANT WITH WALNUTS AND GRAPES

SERVES 2

1 x 1 kg (2 lb) pheasant, prepared for
cooking
salt
freshly ground black pepper
225 g (8 oz) black grapes, halved and
seeded
50 g (2 oz) walnuts, chopped
25 g (1 oz) butter
150 ml (¼ pint) dry white wine
150 ml (¼ pint) double cream
2 egg yolks
sprigs of watercress, to garnish

Power setting: Full/Maximum
Preparation and cooking time: about
50 minutes

1. Preheat a large lidded browning dish on full/maximum power for 5 minutes (or according to the manufacturer's instructions).
2. Season the pheasant with salt and pepper to taste and stuff with two thirds of the grapes and walnuts. Secure the opening with wooden cocktail sticks.
3. Add the butter to the browning dish and swirl quickly to melt. Add the pheasant and roll quickly on all sides to brown evenly. Cover and cook on medium power for 22 minutes, turning over once after 12 minutes. (If the dish is shallow and the lid will not fit with the pheasant in position then cover with greaseproof paper.)
4. Remove the pheasant from the dish with a slotted spoon and place on a warmed serving plate. Cover with foil and leave to stand for 10 minutes.
5. Meanwhile, add the remaining grapes and walnuts to the dish juices with the wine. Blend the cream with the egg yolks and stir into the sauce, blending well. Cook on full/maximum power for 3–4 minutes, stirring twice, until smooth, creamy and lightly thickened.
6. Serve the pheasant hot with the sauce handed separately. Garnish with watercress sprigs and serve with game chips.

COMBINATION OVENS:
Prepare the pheasant as in Step 2 above. Smear the pheasant with the butter and place on a roasting rack set in a shallow dish. *Combination bake at 200°C on low power for 18–20 minutes, turning over twice.* Remove from the rack and dish and place on a warmed serving plate. Leave to stand, covered with foil, for 10 minutes. Prepare the sauce as in Step 5 above, using the dish juices but increase the cooking time to 3½–4½ minutes.

BRAISED PHEASANT IN CREAM SAUCE

SERVES 2–3

75 g (3 oz) butter
1 x 1.5 kg (3 lb) pheasant, prepared for
cooking
1 teaspoon microwave browning seasoning
(optional)
1 onion, peeled and thinly sliced
300 ml (½ pint) double cream
juice of ½ lemon
salt
freshly ground black pepper
sprigs of watercress, to garnish

Power setting: Full/Maximum
Preparation and cooking time: about
45 minutes

1. Place the butter in a large roasting bag, and loosely secure the end with a piece of string or an elastic band. Cook for 1 minute to melt.
2. Place the pheasant in the roasting bag and sprinkle with the microwave browning seasoning, if used, and turn to coat evenly in the butter.
3. Add the onion to the bag, loosely secure the end as before and place on a plate. Cook for 15 minutes, turning over once.
4. Meanwhile, mix the cream with the lemon juice and salt and pepper to taste. Add to the pheasant, re-tie the bag and cook for a further 8 minutes, turning over once.
5. Leave to stand, in the sealed bag, for 10 minutes.
6. Carefully remove the pheasant from the bag and carve into serving portions. Place on a warmed serving plate and spoon the creamy sauce over and around the bird. Garnish with watercress sprigs and serve at once.

COMBINATION OVENS:
Prepare and cook as above using *microwave only* but increase the cooking times in Step 1 to 1¼ minutes; Step 3 to 18½ minutes and Step 4 to 9½ minutes.

FROM THE LEFT: Braised pheasant in cream sauce; Pheasant with walnuts and grapes

FISH AND SHELLFISH

The microwave excels when it comes to cooking the vast range of fish on offer, be it round or flat, white or oily, canned or fresh. Fish cooked in the microwave retains its moist, flaky texture, fresh, natural flavour and delicate hue giving a mariner's feast of unforgettable dishes. Whether it is steamed, stir-fried or baked, the cooking times are almost unbelievably short.

Sole Véronique (recipe, page 84)

HADDOCK WITH DILL SAUCE

750 g (1¾ lb) haddock fillet
juice of 1 lemon
salt
freshly ground white pepper
3 rashers streaky bacon, rinded
boiling water or fish stock
25 g (1 oz) butter
1 rounded tablespoon plain flour
3 teaspoons chopped fresh dill
150 ml (¼ pint) double cream

Power setting: Full/Maximum
Preparation and cooking time: about
25 minutes

1. Season the haddock fillet with the lemon juice and salt and pepper to taste. Place in a greased shallow cooking dish. Lay the bacon rashers on top. Cover and cook for 12–14 minutes, giving the dish a quarter turn every 3 minutes.
2. Remove the fish and bacon from the dish with a slotted spoon and arrange on a warmed serving dish. Keep warm.
3. Strain the cooking juices into a measuring jug and make up to 300 ml (½ pint) with water or fish stock. Add the butter, flour and 2 teaspoons of the dill, whisking well. Cook for 3 minutes, stirring every 1 minute until smooth and thickened.
4. Add the cream, blending well. Cook for

30 seconds until hot but not boiling. Taste and adjust the seasoning, if necessary, and spoon over and around the fish to serve, garnished with the remaining dill.

COMBINATION OVENS:
Prepare and cook as above using *microwave only* but increase the cooking times in Step 1 to 14–16½ minutes; Step 3 to 3½ minutes and Step 4 to 30–45 seconds.

SPICY FISH KEBABS WITH MANDARIN GINGER SAUCE

750 g (1½ lb) firm, chunky white fish
4 cooked jumbo prawns, shelled
olive oil, for brushing
½ teaspoon chilli powder
½ teaspoon ground paprika
freshly ground black pepper
sprigs of coriander, to garnish

Sauce:
150 ml (¼ pint) unsweetened mandarin or
   orange juice
2 teaspoons grated peeled root ginger
2 tablespoons soy sauce
1 teaspoon brown sugar
2 teaspoons cornflour
2 tablespoons dry sherry
salt
freshly ground black pepper

Power setting: Medium/High and Full/
Maximum
Preparation and cooking time: 15–20
minutes, plus standing

1. Cut the fish into bite–sized cubes and each prawn into 2–3 pieces. Thread the fish and prawns on to 4 large wooden or bamboo skewers. Brush lightly with oil and sprinkle with the chilli powder, paprika and pepper to taste.
2. Place on a roasting rack or plate and cover with greaseproof paper. Cook at medium high power for 8–10 minutes, rearranging twice, until the fish is opaque and cooked. Leave to stand, covered, while preparing the sauce.
3. Place the mandarin juice, ginger, soy sauce, sugar, cornflour, sherry and salt and pepper to taste in a bowl, blending well. Cook on full/maximum power for 2 minutes, stirring 3 times until smooth, clear and thickened. Serve with the fish kebabs, garnished with coriander.

COMBINATION OVENS:
Prepare and cook as above using *microwave only* but increase the cooking times in

Step 2 on medium high power to 9½–11½ minutes and in Step 3 on full/maximum power to 2¼–2½ minutes.

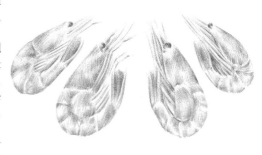

FROM THE LEFT: Spicy fish kebabs with mandarin ginger sauce; Haddock with dill sauce

BAKED MARINATED RED MULLET

4 red mullet, about 200-250 g (7-9 oz)
 each, cleaned and scaled
2 tablespoons lemon juice
3 tablespoons cider vinegar
1 tablespoon clear honey
1 tablespoon oil
120 ml (4 fl oz) dry cider
salt
freshly ground black pepper

To garnish:
lemon slices
radicchio leaves
sprigs of coriander

Power setting: Full/Maximum
Preparation and cooking time: 12
minutes, plus marinating

1. Slash the skin of each fish in 2–3 places and put them in a large shallow dish. Mix the lemon juice, vinegar, honey, oil, cider and salt and pepper to taste. Pour over the fish, cover and leave to marinate for 2–4 hours.
2. Drain the marinade from the fish and discard. Cover and cook for 6–8 minutes, rearranging the fish once and turning the dish twice.
3. Serve hot, garnished with lemon slices, radicchio leaves and some sprigs of fresh coriander.

COMBINATION OVENS:
Prepare and cook as above using *microwave only* but increase the cooking times in Step 2 to 7–9½ minutes, unless your model of combination oven has a grill facility. If it has then you can also choose to cook on *grill high* on the grilling rack for 16 minutes, turning the fish over once.

SKATE WITH CAPER BUTTER

SERVES 3–4
2 x 450 g (1 lb) wings of skate
65 g (2½ oz) butter
1 tablespoon capers
2 tablespoons white wine vinegar
3 tablespoons lemon juice
1 tablespoon chopped fresh parsley
salt
freshly ground black pepper

Power setting: Full/Maximum
Preparation and cooking time: about
20–25 minutes

1. Cut each skate wing into 3 wedges. Place in a large shallow cooking dish. Cover and cook for 5 minutes, turning the dish once.
2. Place the butter in a bowl, cover and cook for 4–5 minutes. Add the capers, vinegar, lemon juice, parsley and salt and pepper to taste, blending well. Cover and cook for 2 minutes.
3. Skin the skate and place in a warmed serving dish. Pour over the caper butter. Cover and cook for 3–4 minutes, turning the dish once. Serve at once.

COMBINATION OVENS:
Prepare and cook as above using *microwave only* but increase the cooking times in Step 1 to 6 minutes; Step 2 to 4½–6 minutes, then 2¼–2½ minutes and Step 3 to 3½–4½ minutes.

Skate is a delicious sea fish which is in season from August to April. Only the triangular wings are found on sale, all ready to cook since the tough black outer skin has usually been removed by the fishmonger. Skate with caper butter is a classic recipe, but monkfish, Dover sole, halibut, plaice and turbot are also delicious cooked in this way.

FROM THE TOP: Baked marinated red mullet; Skate with caper butter

SPICY ORANGE COD STEAKS

2 tablespoons plain flour
¾ teaspoon ground cumin
¾ teaspoon ground turmeric
salt
freshly ground white pepper
4 x 225 g (8 oz) cod steaks
25 g (1 oz) butter
sprigs of fresh parsley, to garnish

Sauce:
25 g (1 oz) butter
grated rind and juice of 2 oranges
150 ml (¼ pint) hot fish stock
150 ml (¼ pint) single cream

Power setting: Full/Maximum
Preparation and cooking time: 15–20
minutes

1. Mix the flour with the cumin, turmeric and salt and pepper to taste. Lightly coat the cod steaks with the mixture, reserving any excess.
2. Place the butter in a large shallow dish and cook for 1 minute to melt. Fold or tuck in the end flaps of the cod steaks and secure to a neat shape with wooden cocktail sticks. Arrange with sticks to the centre of the dish. Cover and cook for 8–9 minutes, rotating the dish twice and turning the fish over once. Leave to stand, covered, while making the sauce.
3. Place the butter, orange rind and juice and remaining flour in a large jug. Cook for 1 minute, stirring once. Gradually add the stock and cook for 2 minutes, stirring once. Add the cream, blend well with salt and pepper to taste. Cook for ½ minute until hot but not boiling.
4. Spoon the sauce over the cod steaks with the creamy orange sauce. Garnish with fresh parsley and serve with rice and a salad, if liked.

COMBINATION OVENS:
Prepare and cook as above using *microwave only* but increase the cooking times in Step 2 to 1–1¼ minutes then 9½–10½ minutes and Step 3 to 1–1¼ minutes, 2–2½ minutes then ½–¾ minute.

SCAMPI PROVENÇALE

25 g (1 oz) butter
1 onion, peeled and chopped
1 garlic clove, peeled and chopped
1 x 400 g (14 oz) can peeled tomatoes, drained
5 tablespoons dry white wine
pinch of sugar
1 tablespoon chopped fresh coriander
salt
freshly ground black pepper
450 g (1 lb) peeled uncooked scampi
sprigs of fresh coriander, to garnish

Power setting: Full/Maximum
Preparation and cooking time: 20
minutes

1. Place the butter in a bowl and cook for 1 minute. Add the onion and garlic, blending well. Cover and cook for 3 minutes, stirring once.
2. Add the tomatoes, wine, sugar, coriander and salt and pepper to taste, blending well. Cover and cook for 3 minutes, stirring once.
3. Add the scampi, blending well. Cover and cook for 4–5 minutes, stirring once.
4. Garnish and serve hot with boiled rice and a crisp green salad.

COMBINATION OVENS:
Prepare and cook as above using *microwave only* but increase the cooking times in Step 1 to 1–1¼ minutes then 3½ minutes; Step 2 to 3½ minutes and Step 4 to 4½–6 minutes.

Scampi (also known as Dublin Bay prawns and langoustines) are prized shellfish that are best bought whole and uncooked – the heads and shells will make delicious stock for a fish soup. Alternatively buy uncooked frozen tails and defrost and peel them. To defrost uncooked frozen tails in the microwave allow about 5–6 minutes on Defrost per 450 g (1 lb) of scampi, then leave to stand for 5–10 minutes until thawed completely.

FROM THE LEFT: Spicy orange cod steaks; Scampi Provençale

STIR-FRIED MONKFISH

1 tablespoon sesame oil
750 g (1½ lb) monkfish tail fillets, boned
  and thinly sliced
225 g (8 oz) white cabbage, shredded
1 small red pepper, cored, seeded and
  chopped
1 small green pepper, cored, seeded and
  chopped
1 small onion, peeled and chopped
100 g (4 oz) fresh beansprouts
1–2 tablespoons soy sauce
pinch of Chinese 5-spice powder

Power setting: Full/Maximum
Preparation and cooking time: about
35–40 minutes

1. Preheat a browning dish for 6 minutes (or according to the manufacturer's instructions). Add the oil and swirl to coat. Add the fish and cook for 4–5 minutes, stirring twice. Remove the fish with a slotted spoon and set aside.
2. Reheat the browning dish for 3 minutes. Add the cabbage, peppers and onion, blending well. Cook for 4 minutes, stirring twice.
3. Add the beansprouts and monkfish, blending well. Cook for 2 minutes, stirring once.
4. Add soy sauce and 5-spice powder to taste. Serve at once.

COMBINATION OVENS:
Prepare and cook as above using *microwave only* but increase the cooking times in Step 1 to 7 minutes, then 4½–6 minutes; Step 2 to 3½ minutes, then 4¾ minutes and Step 3 to 2¼–2½ minutes.

DEVONSHIRE COD

SERVES 2
2 x 225 g (8 oz) cod steaks
150 ml (¼ pint) dry cider
salt
freshly ground black pepper
1 tomato, peeled and sliced
25 g (1 oz) mushrooms, wiped and chopped
25 g (1 oz) butter
1 tablespoon cornflour
50 g (2 oz) Cheddar or Double Gloucester
  cheese, grated
450 g (1 lb) creamed potatoes
sprigs of fennel, to garnish

Power setting: Full/Maximum
Preparation and cooking time: about
30–35 minutes

1. Place the cod in a shallow casserole dish. Pour over the cider and season with salt and pepper to taste. Top with the tomato and mushrooms and dot with half of the butter. Cover and cook for 5 minutes, turning the dish once.
2. Carefully strain the juices from the fish and make up to 150 ml (¼ pint) with extra cider, if necessary.
3. Place the remaining butter in a jug and cook for 30 seconds to melt. Gradually add the cornflour and reserved juices, blending well. Cook for 2 minutes, stirring twice, until smooth and thickened. Pour over the fish and sprinkle with the cheese.
4. Pipe the creamed potatoes in a decorative border around the fish. Cook for 2 minutes, turning the dish once. Garnish and serve hot.

COMBINATION OVENS:
Prepare and cook as above using *microwave only* but increase the cooking times in Step 1 to 6 minutes; Step 3 to 30–45 seconds, then 2–2½ minutes and Step 4 for 2½ minutes. If liked, the recipe can be prepared up to the end of Step 3, the potatoes piped around the fish, then *combination bake* at 250°C using *low* power for 3–5 minutes until the cheese is bubbly and the potato is tinged golden.

FROM THE TOP: Stir-fried monkfish; Devonshire cod

BARBECUE BACON TROUT

4 trout fillets
8 rashers streaky bacon, rinded
4 tablespoons tomato ketchup
4 teaspoons brown sugar
4 teaspoons French mustard
sprigs of tarragon, to garnish

Power setting: Full/Maximum
Preparation and cooking time: 20–25
minutes

1. Place the trout fillets in a cooking dish and cover with the bacon. Cover with absorbent paper towels and cook for 6 minutes, turning the dish once.
2. Meanwhile, blend the tomato ketchup with the sugar and mustard. Brush evenly over the trout and bacon and cook, uncovered, for 3–4 minutes.
3. Garnish and serve hot with a crisp salad.

COMBINATION OVENS:

Prepare and cook as above using *microwave only* but increase the cooking times in Step 1 to 7 minutes and Step 2 to 3½–4½ minutes.

Some microwave cookers have a grill facility for cooking small cuts of meat, poultry and fish. If you wish to use one for this recipe, then simply place the trout in a shallow flameproof dish and cover with the bacon. Cook with the grill setting on high for 12 minutes, turning the fish over once after 6 minutes. Spoon the barbecue sauce mixture over the fish and cook for a further 3–4 minutes until crisped and bubbly.

SCALLOPS WITH CIDER AND CREAM

50 g (2 oz) butter
2 shallots, peeled and finely chopped
40 g (1½ oz) plain flour
5 tablespoons dry cider
5 tablespoons milk
100 g (4 oz) mushrooms, wiped and sliced
450 g (1 lb) scallops, prepared for cooking
salt
freshly ground white pepper
2 tablespoons double cream
25 g (1 oz) cheese, grated
chopped fresh parsley, to garnish

Power setting: Full/Maximum
Preparation and cooking time: about
30–35 minutes

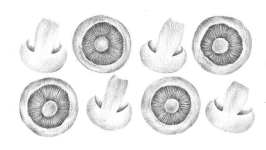

Scallops, like oysters, are at their best when there is an 'R' in the month, and again, like oysters, they are a wonderful treat but, sadly, at an equally wonderful price. If you ever buy them unopened, place them under a hot grill for 1–1½ minutes until the shells start to open up, then it is quite simple to prise them open.
1. Place the butter and shallots in a large cooking dish. Cover and cook for 3 minutes, stirring once. Add the flour, blending well. Cook for 1 minute, stirring once.
2. Gradually add the cider and milk,

blending well. Stir in the mushrooms, scallops and salt and pepper to taste. Cover and cook for 5–6 minutes, stirring 3 times until the scallops are cooked and coated in a creamy sauce.
3. Add the cream and cheese, blending well. Cover and cook for 2–3 minutes, stirring once.
4. Serve hot in individual scallop shells or small dishes. Sprinkle with chopped parsley to serve.

COMBINATION OVENS:

Prepare and cook as above using *microwave only* but increase the cooking times in Step 1 to 3½ minutes and 1–1¼ minutes; Step 2 to 6–7 minutes and Step 3 to 2½–3½ minutes.

FROM THE LEFT: Scallops with cider and cream; Barbecue bacon trout

SALMON AND GREEN BEAN STIR-FRY

SERVES 2–3
2 x 175 g (6 oz) salmon steaks
15 g (½ oz) melted butter
1 tablespoon oil
350 g (12 oz) thin French beans, topped
and tailed and halved
100 g (4 oz) mushrooms, wiped and sliced
2 carrots, peeled and sliced into julienne
strips
3 teaspoons lemon juice
2 tablespoons dry white wine
¼ teaspoon grated lemon rind
pinch of mustard powder
freshly ground black pepper
75 g (3 oz) cashew nuts

Power setting: Full/Maximum
Preparation and cooking time: 10–15
minutes

1. Arrange the salmon steaks in a shallow dish so that the tail ends are to the centre of the dish. Brush with the melted butter, cover with greaseproof paper and cook for 3–3½ minutes, rearranging or turning once. Leave to stand for 5 minutes, then remove the flesh from the bone, skin and flake into bite–sized pieces.
2. Place the oil in a large shallow dish and cook for 1 minute.
3. Add the beans, mushrooms and carrots, blending well. Cover and cook for 3 minutes, stirring once.
4. Meanwhile, sprinkle the salmon with 1 teaspoon of the lemon juice. Mix the wine with the remaining lemon juice and the lemon rind and add mustard and pepper to taste.
5. Add the wine mixture to the vegetables, blending well. Cook, uncovered, for 2 minutes until the vegetables are just tender but still crisp.
6. Add the salmon and cashew nuts,

blending well. Cook for 30 seconds–1 minute until hot and serve at once with cooked rice or pasta.

COMBINATION OVENS:
Prepare and cook as above using *microwave only* but increase the cooking times in Step 1 to 3½–4½ minutes; Step 2 to 1–1¼ minutes; Step 3 to 3½ minutes; Step 5 to 2¼–2½ minutes and Step 6 to ¾ to 1 minute.

SMOKED HADDOCK MORNAY

450 g (1 lb) smoked haddock fillets
65 g (2½ oz) butter
2 teaspoons lemon juice
50 g (2 oz) plain flour
600 ml (1 pint) milk
2 egg yolks, beaten
100 g (4 oz) Cheddar cheese, grated
4 teaspoons capers, chopped
salt
freshly ground black pepper
sprigs of parsley, to garnish

Power setting: Full/Maximum
Preparation and cooking time: about
20 minutes

FROM THE TOP: Salmon and green bean stir-fry;
Smoked haddock mornay

1. Arrange the fish fillets in a large dish with the thicker portions to the outside of the dish. Dot with 15 g (½ oz) of the butter and sprinkle with the lemon juice. Cover and cook for 5–6 minutes, rearranging once. Leave to stand, covered, while preparing the sauce.
2. Place the remaining butter in a large heatproof jug or bowl and cook for 1 minute to melt. Blend in the flour, milk and any juices from the haddock. Cook for 4–6 minutes, stirring every 2 minutes until smooth, boiling and thickened. Add the egg yolks, 75 g (3 oz) of the grated Cheddar cheese, the capers and salt and pepper to taste, blending well.
3. Flake the smoked haddock, removing and discarding any skin and bones and

fold into the sauce.
4. Spoon into a flameproof dish and sprinkle with the remaining cheese. Cook for 1½–2 minutes to reheat until bubbly.
5. Brown under a preheated hot grill, if liked, before serving garnished with parsley sprigs. Serve with crusty bread or toast fingers.

COMBINATION OVENS:
Prepare and cook as above using *microwave only* to the end of Step 3 but increase the cooking times in Step 1 to 6–7 minutes and Step 2 to 4½–7 minutes. Spoon the mixture into an ovenproof dish and then sprinkle with the remaining cheese. *Combination bake* at 250°C using *low* power for 5–8 minutes until crisp and golden.

TICKLED TROUT

40 g (1½ oz) butter
½ small onion, peeled and chopped
75 g (3 oz) dried white breadcrumbs
1 teaspoon chopped fresh sage
salt
freshly ground black pepper
225 g (8 oz) button mushrooms, wiped and
  sliced
5 tablespoons single cream
4 x 225–275 g (8–10 oz) trout, cleaned
sprigs of mint, to garnish

Power setting: Full/Maximum
Preparation and cooking time: 20
minutes

1. Place the butter in a large shallow dish. Add the onion and cook for 2 minutes. Add the breadcrumbs and sage, blending well. Cook, uncovered, for 2–3 minutes, until lightly browned and crisp, stirring three times. Season with salt and pepper to taste.
2. Place the mushrooms and cream in a bowl and cook, uncovered, for 3 minutes, stirring once.
3. Arrange the trout in a shallow serving dish. Slash the skin in 2–3 places to prevent bursting. Cover and cook for 7–9 minutes, turning the dish once.
4. Spoon over the mushroom mixture and sprinkle with the herbed breadcrumbs. Cook, uncovered, for a further 2 minutes until hot and bubbly. Serve at once, garnished with mint sprigs.

COMBINATION OVENS:
Prepare and cook as above using *microwave only* but increase the cooking times in Step 1 to 2¼–2½ minutes, then 2½–3½ minutes; Step 2 to 3½ minutes; Step 3 to 8–10½ minutes and Step 4 to 2¼–2½ minutes.

SOLE VÉRONIQUE

2 soles, filleted and skinned
1 small onion, peeled and sliced
4 button mushrooms, wiped and sliced
3 sprigs parsley
1 bay leaf
salt
freshly ground white pepper
150 ml (¼ pint) dry white wine
25 g (1 oz) butter
25 g (1 oz) plain flour
150 ml (¼ pint) milk
1 teaspoon lemon juice
175 g (6 oz) white grapes, peeled, halved
  and pips removed
2 tablespoons double cream
chives, to garnish

Power setting: Full/Maximum
Preparation and cooking time: about
30–35 minutes

1. Place the sole fillets in a cooking dish with the onion, mushrooms, parsley, bay leaf, salt and pepper to taste and wine. Cover and cook for 4–4½ minutes, turning the dish once.
2. Drain, reserving the stock. Remove and discard the onion, mushrooms, parsley and bay leaf. Place the fish on a warmed serving plate and keep warm.

3. Place the butter in a bowl and cook for ½ minute to melt. Add the flour, blending well. Gradually add the reserved stock and milk, blending well. Cook for 3–4 minutes, stirring every 1 minute until smooth and thickened.
4. Add the lemon juice, two-thirds of the grapes and the cream, blending well. Pour over the fish and cook for 2–2½ minutes, turning the dish once.
5. Serve garnished with chives and the remaining grapes.

COMBINATION OVENS:
Prepare and cook as above using *microwave only* but increase the cooking times in Step 1 to 4½–5¼ minutes; Step 3 to 30–45 seconds, then 3½–4½ minutes and Step 4 to 2½–3 minutes.

FROM THE LEFT: Tickled trout; Sole Véronique

PASTA, RICE AND PULSES

Tender yet al dente pasta, fluffy boiled rice with each grain separate, and perfectly cooked pulses and grains are the guaranteed promises of the microwave oven, even though time savings over conventional methods are minimal. The bonuses, however, are numerous; there are no sticky pans, no steamy kitchens, little risk of over-cooking and you can cut down on washing up by cooking and serving in the same dish.

Tortellini in creamy pesto sauce (recipe, page 96)

PIQUANT PASTA

SERVES 2
175 g (6 oz) fettucine or narrow ribbon
  noodles
900 ml (1½ pints) boiling water
7 teaspoons olive oil
2 garlic cloves, peeled and crushed
1 small chilli, seeded and chopped
2 tablespoons chopped fresh parsley
salt
freshly ground black pepper
lettuce, to garnish

Power setting: Full/Maximum
Preparation and cooking time: about 10
minutes

1. Place the pasta in a large bowl with the
water and 1 teaspoon of the oil. Cover and
cook for 6 minutes, stirring twice. Leave to
stand, covered, while preparing the garlic
mixture.
2. Place the remaining oil, garlic and chilli
in a small bowl. Cover and cook for 2–3
minutes, until the garlic and chilli are softened (but do not let the garlic brown).

3. Drain the pasta and place in a warm
serving dish. Add the garlic and chilli oil,
parsley and salt and pepper to taste and
toss to mix. Garnish and serve at once.

COMBINATION OVENS:
Prepare and cook as above using *microwave only* but increase the cooking times in
Step 1 to 7 minutes and Step 2 to 2½–3½
minutes.

VEGETABLE RISOTTO

1 tablespoon oil
1 large onion, peeled and sliced
225 g (8 oz) long-grain rice
1 x 275 g (10 oz) packet frozen stir-fry
  vegetables or 275 g (10 oz) chopped mixed
  vegetables, e.g. peas, sweetcorn kernels,
  cauliflower florets, diced carrots
600 ml (1 pint) boiling chicken or vegetable
  stock
1 teaspoon dried marjoram
salt
freshly ground black pepper
50 g (2 oz) mature Cheddar cheese, grated

To garnish:
celery leaves
sprigs of parsley

Power setting: Full/Maximum and
Medium
Preparation and cooking time: about
25 minutes

1. Place the oil, onion and rice in a large
bowl. Cook on full/maximum power for 3
minutes, stirring once.
2. Add the vegetables, cover and cook on
full/maximum power for 2 minutes (if
using fresh vegetables then cook on full/
maximum power for 4 minutes), stirring
once.
3. Add the stock, marjoram and salt and
pepper to taste, blending well. Cover and
cook on full/maximum power for 3 minutes. Reduce the power setting to medium
and cook for a further 12 minutes, stirring
once. Leave to stand, covered, for 5
minutes.
4. Spoon into a warm serving dish and
sprinkle with the cheese, garnish and serve
at once.

COMBINATION OVENS:
Prepare and cook as above using *microwave only* but increase the cooking times in

Step 1 on full/maximum power to 3½
minutes; Step 2 on full/maximum power
to 2½ minutes (or if using fresh vegetables
to 4¾ minutes) and Step 3 on full/maxi-
mum to 3½ minutes, then on medium to
14 minutes.

FROM THE TOP: Piquant pasta; Vegetable risotto

PASTA QUILLS WITH CHEESE AND BACON

350 g (12 oz) pasta quills
1.75 litres (3 pints) boiling water
1 teaspoon oil
100 g (4 oz) unsmoked streaky bacon, rinded
225 g (8oz) Cheddar or Double Gloucester cheese, grated
4–5 tablespoons milk or cream
salt
freshly ground black pepper

Power setting: Full/Maximum and Medium
Preparation and cooking time: about 25 minutes

1. Place the pasta in a large bowl with the water and oil. Cover and cook on full/maximum power for 12–14 minutes, stirring once. Leave to stand, covered, while preparing the sauce.
2. Place the bacon on a plate lined with absorbent paper towels and cook on full/maximum power for 3½–4 minutes, or until cooked and crispy. Allow to cool slightly then chop or crumble into small pieces.
3. Place the cheese and milk or cream in a bowl. Cook on medium power for 4–5 minutes until the cheese is smooth and melted, stirring twice. Season to taste with salt and pepper.
4. Drain the pasta quills, add the cheese and toss to coat. If necessary cook the mixture on full/maximum power for 1–2 minutes to ensure that the pasta and sauce are hot enough to mix smoothly. Place the mixture in a warm serving dish and sprinkle with the bacon. Serve at once with a crisp salad.

COMBINATION OVENS:
Prepare and cook as above using microwave only, but increase the cooking times in Step 1 on full/maximum power to 14–16½ minutes; Step 2 on full/maximum power to 4–4½ minutes; Step 3 on medium power to 4½ minutes and Step 4 on full/maximum to 1¼-2½ minutes.

SPAGHETTI GORGONZOLA

SERVES 2
175 g (6 oz) spaghetti
900 ml (1½ pints) boiling water
1 teaspoon oil
120 ml (4 fl oz) single cream
100 g (4 oz) Gorgonzola cheese, crumbled
salt
freshly ground black pepper
25 g (1 oz) butter
pinch of ground nutmeg
2 spring onions, trimmed and chopped
25 g (1 oz) grated Parmesan cheese
snipped chives, to garnish

Power setting: Full/Maximum
Preparation and cooking time: 15–20 minutes

1. Place the spaghetti in a large bowl with the water and oil. Allow it to soften, then submerge it entirely. Cover and cook for 10–12 minutes, stirring once. Leave to stand, covered, while preparing the sauce.
2. Place the cream and Gorgonzola in a bowl. Cook for 2–3 minutes, stirring twice, until smooth and melted. Add salt and pepper to taste, blending well.
3. Drain the spaghetti and toss with the butter, nutmeg, spring onions and Parmesan cheese. Place in a warmed serving dish and pour over the sauce. Sprinkle with snipped chives and serve at once with a tomato and basil salad.

COMBINATION OVENS:
Prepare and cook as above using *microwave only* but increase the cooking times in Step 1 to 11½–14 minutes and Step 2 to 2½–3½ minutes.

FROM THE TOP: Pasta quills with cheese and bacon; Spaghetti Gorgonzola

TAGLIATELLE WITH MUSHROOM SAUCE

350 g (12 oz) tagliatelle verde
1.2 litres (2 pints) boiling water
1 teaspoon oil
225 g (8 oz) bacon, rinded and chopped
100 g (4 oz) mushrooms, wiped and sliced
25 g (1 oz) butter
25 g (1 oz) plain flour
300 ml (½ pint) milk
salt
freshly ground black pepper

Power setting: Full/Maximum
Preparation and cooking time: 20–25 minutes

1. Place the tagliatelle in a bowl with the water and oil. Cover and cook for 6 minutes, stirring once. Leave to stand, covered, while preparing the sauce.
2. Place the bacon in a bowl, cover and cook for 6 minutes, stirring once. Remove with a slotted spoon and drain on absorbent paper towels.

3. Add the mushrooms to the bacon fat, blending well. Cover and cook for 2 minutes.
4. Place the butter in a bowl and cook for ½ minute to melt. Add the flour, blending well. Gradually add the milk and cook for 3–4 minutes, stirring every 1 minute until smooth, boiling and thickened. Stir in the bacon, mushrooms with their juice and salt and pepper to taste.
5. Drain the tagliatelle and place in a warm serving dish. Spoon the sauce over and serve at once.

COMBINATION OVENS:
Prepare and cook as above using *microwave only* but increase the cooking times in Step 1 to 7 minutes; in Step 2 to 7 minutes and Step 4 to 3½–4½ minutes.

SPICED LENTILS

225 g (8 oz) continental lentils
900 ml (1½ pints) boiling water or
 vegetable stock
1 tablespoon oil
1 onion, peeled and sliced
1–2 garlic cloves, peeled and crushed
1 green pepper, cored, seeded and chopped
4 tomatoes, peeled and quartered
100 g (4 oz) mushrooms, wiped and
 chopped
½ teaspoon chilli powder
½ teaspoon ground coriander
salt
freshly ground black pepper
4 slices of French bread
2 oz (50 g) Edam cheese, sliced

Power setting: Full/Maximum
Preparation and cooking time: 30–35 minutes

FROM THE TOP: Tagliatelle with mushroom sauce; Spiced lentils

1. Place the lentils in a large bowl with the water or stock. Cover and cook for 20–25 minutes, until tender, stirring once. Drain the lentils, if necessary.
2. Place the oil, onion, garlic and green pepper in a bowl. Cover and cook for 4 minutes, stirring once.
3. Add the tomatoes, mushrooms, chilli powder, ground coriander and salt and pepper to taste. Cover and cook for 3 minutes, stirring once.
4. Add to the cooked lentils, blending well, then spoon the mixture into 4 individual serving dishes.
5. Meanwhile, cover the bread slices with the cheese and grill conventionally until golden and bubbly. Arrange the bread and cheese topping on top of the lentil mixture and serve at once.

COMBINATION OVENS:
Prepare and cook as above using *micro-wave only* to the end of Step 4 but increase the cooking times in Step 1 to 23–29 minutes; Step 2 to 4½ minutes and Step 3 to 3½ minutes, then top with the bread slices and *combination bake* at 220°C using *low* power for 5 minutes or until the cheese is golden and bubbly.

SPICED CHICK PEAS WITH FRUIT AND VEGETABLES

SERVES 4–6

175 g (6 oz) chick peas, soaked in cold
water for 6–8 hours and drained
boiling water or vegetable stock
1 tablespoon oil
1 onion, peeled and chopped
4 sticks celery, scrubbed and chopped
1 tablespoon plain flour
1 tablespoon curry powder
200 ml (7 fl oz) hot vegetable stock
1 teaspoon ground ginger
grated rind and juice of 1 lemon
1 x 400 g (14 oz) can apricot halves,
drained
2 bananas, peeled and thickly sliced
225 g (8 oz) cooking apples, peeled, cored
and quartered
50 g (2 oz) raisins
150 ml (¼ pint) soured cream

Power setting: Full/Maximum and
Medium
Preparation and cooking time: about
55 minutes, plus soaking

1. Place the drained chick peas in a large bowl and cover with water or vegetable stock. Cover and cook on full/maximum power for 10 minutes. Reduce the power setting to medium and cook for a further 20–25 minutes, adding extra boiling water or vegetable stock to cover, if needed, stirring twice, until tender. Drain thoroughly.
2. Place the oil, onion and celery in a large casserole dish. Cover and cook on full/ maximum power for 5 minutes, stirring once.
3. Add the flour and curry powder, blending well and cook on full/maximum power for 1 minute.
4. Gradually add the stock, ginger, lemon rind and lemon juice, blending well. Cook on full/maximum power for 3 minutes, stirring every 1 minute until smooth and thickened.
5. Add the apricots, bananas, apples and raisins, blending well. Cover and cook on full/maximum power for 3 minutes, stirring once.

6. Add the cooked chick peas, blending well. Cover and cook on full/maximum power for a further 3–4 minutes or until the vegetables and fruit are hot and just tender. Swirl in the soured cream and serve at once with a bowl of cooked rice.

COMBINATION OVENS:
Prepare and cook as above using *microwave only* but increase the cooking times in Step 1 on full/maximum power to 11½ minutes then on medium power to 23–29 minutes; Step 2 on full/maximum power to 6 minutes; Step 3 on full/maximum power to 1–1¼ minutes; Step 4 on full/ maximum power to 3½ minutes; Step 5 on full/maximum power to 3½ minutes and Step 6 on full/maximum power to 3½–4½ minutes.

HOT BEAN SALAD

225 g (8 oz) dried mixed borlotti, red
kidney or cannellini beans, soaked in cold
water for 6–8 hours
boiling water or vegetable stock
225 g (8 oz) French beans, topped, tailed,
and cut into 2.5 cm (1 inch) pieces
1 small onion, peeled and thinly sliced
1 clove garlic, peeled and crushed
4 tablespoons vinaigrette dressing
2 tablespoons chopped fresh parsley

Power setting: Full/Maximum and
Medium
Preparation and cooking time: about
50 minutes, plus soaking

1. Drain the soaked beans, place in a cooking dish and cover with boiling water or vegetable stock. Cover and cook on full/ maximum power for 10 minutes. Reduce the power setting to medium and cook for a further 20–25 minutes, adding extra boiling water or vegetable stock to cover, if needed, stirring twice, until tender. Drain thoroughly.
2. Place the French beans, onion, garlic and salad dressing in a bowl. Cover and cook on full/maximum power for 6–8 minutes or until the vegetables are tender– crisp, stirring once.
3. Add the cooked dried beans with the

parsley, blending well. Cover and cook on full/maximum power for 2 minutes to reheat. Serve at once.

COMBINATION OVENS:
Prepare and cook as above using *microwave only* but increase the cooking times in Step 1 on full/maximum power to 11½ minutes, then on medium power to 23–29 minutes; Step 2 on full/maximum power to 7–9½ minutes and Step 3 on full/maximum power to 2½ minutes.

FROM THE LEFT: Spiced chick peas with fruit and vegetables; Hot bean salad

SPAGHETTI WITH TUNA FISH AND PRAWN SAUCE

225 g (8 oz) spaghetti
1.2 litres (2 pints) boiling water
1 teaspoon oil
1 onion, peeled and finely chopped
1 garlic clove, peeled and crushed
1 teaspoon cornflour
1 x 225 g (8 oz) can peeled tomatoes,
   chopped
1 teaspoon chilli powder
2 tablespoons tomato purée
1 x 200 g (7 oz) can tuna fish in brine,
   drained and flaked
100 g (4 oz) peeled prawns
salt
freshly ground black pepper
sprigs of dill, to garnish

Power setting: Full/Maximum
Preparation and cooking time: 20–25
minutes

1. Place the spaghetti in a large bowl with the water and oil. Allow it to soften, then submerge it entirely. Cover and cook for 10–12 minutes, stirring once. Leave to stand, covered, while preparing the sauce.
2. Place the onion and garlic in a bowl. Cover and cook for 3 minutes. Add the cornflour, tomatoes, chilli powder, tomato purée, tuna fish, prawns and salt and pepper to taste, blending well. Cook, uncovered, for 4 minutes, stirring once.
3. Drain the spaghetti and arrange on a warm serving plate. Spoon over the tuna fish and prawn sauce. Garnish with sprigs of dill and serve immediately.

COMBINATION OVENS:
Prepare and cook as above using *microwave only* but increase the cooking times in Step 1 to 11½–14 minutes and Step 2 to 3½ then 4½ minutes.

TORTELLINI IN CREAMY PESTO SAUCE

SERVES 2
175 g (6 oz) tortellini
900 ml (1½ pints) boiling water
1 teaspoon oil
150 ml (¼ pint) single cream
1 tablespoon canned or bottled pesto sauce
salt
freshly ground black pepper
grated Parmesan cheese

Power setting: Full/Maximum
Preparation and cooking time: 15–20
minutes

1. Place the tortellini in a bowl with the water and oil. Cover and cook for 12–14 minutes, stirring once. Leave to stand, covered, while preparing the sauce.
2. Place the cream in a bowl and cook for 1½ minutes. Add the pesto sauce and salt and pepper to taste, blending well.
3. Drain the tortellini and add to the sauce, Toss well to coat in the sauce. Spoon into a warm serving dish and sprinkle with grated Parmesan cheese. Serve with a crisp green salad.

COMBINATION OVENS:
Prepare and cook as above using *microwave only* but increase the cooking times in Step 1 to 14–16½ minutes and Step 2 to 1½–2 minutes.

All the instructions and timings given for cooking pasta in this chapter are for the dried variety. If you want to use fresh pasta remember that the cooking times will be reduced considerably. In most cases place the pasta in a bowl with boiling water to cover, then cook on full/maximum for two-thirds of the conventional cooking time stated on the packet instructions. Cover and leave to stand for 3–5 minutes, then drain and serve.

FROM THE TOP: Spaghetti with tuna fish and prawn sauce; Tortellini in creamy pesto sauce

PUDDINGS AND DESSERTS

If you've neglected serving puddings through
lack of time then you'll welcome the return of
cool fools, crunchy fruit-filled crumbles and
light-as-air sponges with piping hot sauces.
The microwave means that many sweet treats
can be cooked while you're enjoying a main
meal, and many more can be speedily prepared
well in advance.

Cinnamon baked pears (recipe, page 104)

AUTUMN BRAMBLE PUDDING

SERVES 6–8

*450 g (1 lb) dessert apples, peeled cored and
  chopped*
450 g (1 lb) blackberries, hulled
*225 g (8 oz) fresh or frozen redcurrants
  (thawed if frozen), topped and tailed*
100–175 g (4–6 oz) sugar
2 tablespoons water
2 teaspoons powdered gelatine
*6–8 slices brown bread, crusts removed, or
  about 16 trifle sponges, sliced*
sprig of redcurrants, to decorate

Power setting: Full/Maximum
Preparation and cooking time: about
20 minutes, plus chilling

1. Place the apples in a bowl. Cover and cook for 5 minutes, stirring once.
2. Add the blackberries, redcurrants and sugar, blending well. Cover and cook for 2–3 minutes until just softened.
3. Place the water in a bowl and sprinkle over the gelatine. Leave for about 3–5 minutes until spongy. Cook for 30–45 seconds, until the gelatine is clear and dissolved, then stir into the fruit mixture.
4. Meanwhile, line the bottom and sides of a 1.5 litre (2½ pint) pudding basin with the bread or trifle sponge slices, trimming them to fit neatly.
5. Layer the fruit and the remaining bread or trifle sponges in the basin, finishing with a layer of bread or sponge.
6. Cover the pudding with a plate and put a heavy weight on top to press the fruit down firmly. Chill for about 6–8 hours or until the juices soak through the bread or sponge.
7. To serve, turn the pudding out on to a serving dish, decorate with a sprig of redcurrants and serve with plain yogurt.

COMBINATION OVENS:
Prepare and cook as above using *microwave only* but increase the cooking times in Step 1 to 6 minutes; Step 2 to 2½–3½ minutes and Step 3 to 45 seconds–1 minute.

BLACKCURRANT BAKED CHEESECAKE

SERVES 8

Base:
50 g (2 oz) butter
*175 g (6 oz) wheatmeal digestive biscuits,
  crushed*

Filling:
50 g (2 oz) butter
50 g (2 oz) sugar
225 g (8 oz) cream cheese
150 ml (¼ pint) soured cream
2 eggs, separated
*1 x 400 g (14 oz) can blackcurrant pie
  filling*
sprig of mint, to decorate

Power setting: Full/Maximum
Preparation and cooking time: about
20 minutes, plus chilling

1. To make the base, place the butter in a bowl and cook for 1 minute to melt. Add the biscuit crumbs and stir to coat. Spoon on to the base of a 23 cm (9 inch) deep flan or cake dish, pressing down well.
2. To make the filling, cream the butter with the sugar until light and fluffy. Slowly beat in the cream cheese, soured cream and egg yolks, blending together well.
3. Whisk the egg whites until they stand in stiff peaks and fold into the cream mixture with a metal spoon. Pour on top of the prepared base and cook for 8 minutes, giving the dish a quarter turn every 2 minutes. Leave to stand until cool, then chill thoroughly.
4. When cool, top the cheesecake with the pie filling and decorate with a mint sprig, if liked. Serve lightly chilled.

COMBINATION OVENS:
Prepare and cook as above using *microwave only* to the end of Step 2 but increase the cooking time in Step 1 to 1–1¼ minutes. Pour the prepared cheesecake mixture over the base and *combination bake* at 190°C using *high* power for 5 minutes, then *low* for 10–12 minutes. Cool, then chill thoroughly. Proceed from Step 4 above.

FROM THE TOP: Autumn bramble pudding; Blackcurrant baked cheesecake

LEMON SOUFFLÉ

SERVES 4–6

1 tablespoon powdered gelatine
2 tablespoons water
150 g (5 oz) caster sugar
200 ml (7 fl oz) hot water
pinch of salt
3 eggs, separated
grated rind and juice of 1 large lemon
200 ml (7 fl oz) double cream

To decorate:
whipped cream
lemon butterflies

Power setting: Full/Maximum and Defrost
Preparation and cooking time: about 40 minutes, plus chilling

1. Lightly grease a 600 ml (1 pint) soufflé dish. Cut a double strip of greaseproof paper, equal in width to the height of the dish plus 5 cm (2 inches) and long enough to go right round the outside of the dish. Lightly grease the top 5 cm (2 inches) and tie securely with string around the outside of the dish, greased side inside.
2. Sprinkle the gelatine over the 2 tablespoons water in a small bowl and leave to soften. Cook on full/maximum power for 15–20 seconds to dissolve.
3. Mix 100 g (4 oz) of the sugar with the dissolved gelatine, hot water, salt and egg yolks, blending well. Cook on defrost power for 6–9 minutes, or until the mixture almost reaches boiling point (but do not allow to boil), stirring every 2 minutes.
4. Add the lemon rind and juice, blending well. Leave to cool and thicken but not set.
5. Whisk the egg whites until they stand in stiff peaks. Whisk in the remaining sugar until firm and glossy.

6. Whip the cream until it stands in soft peaks. Fold into the lemon mixture with the egg whites using a metal spoon. Pour into the prepared soufflé dish and chill to set.
7. Before serving, carefully ease the greaseproof paper away from the soufflé using the back of a knife. Decorate with rosettes of whipped cream and lemon butterflies.

COMBINATION OVENS:
Prepare and cook as above using *microwave only*, but increase the cooking time in Step 3 to 7-10½ minutes.

PLUM AND APPLE FOOL

SERVES 4–6

450 g (1 lb) plums, halved and stoned
1 large dessert apple, peeled, cored and sliced
1 teaspoon grated lemon rind
2 tablespoons apple fruit syrup or water
1½ tablespoons custard powder
2 tablespoons caster sugar
300 ml (½ pint) skimmed milk
150 ml (¼ pint) whipping cream

Power setting: Full/Maximum
Preparation and cooking time: 15 minutes, plus chilling

1. Place the plums, apple, lemon rind and apple fruit syrup or water in a bowl. Cover and cook for 6 minutes until the fruit is very tender, stirring once. Purée in a blender or pass through a fine nylon sieve.
2. Meanwhile, mix the custard powder with the sugar and milk in a large jug or bowl. Cook for 3–4 minutes, stirring every

minute until smooth, boiling and thickened. Stir in the plum and apple purée, cover and leave until cold.
3. Whip the cream until it stands in soft peaks then fold gently into the fruit and custard mixture until the fool has a streaked appearance. Spoon into serving glasses and serve, lightly chilled.

COMBINATION OVENS:
Prepare and cook as above using *microwave only* but increase the cooking times in Step 1 to 7 minutes and in Step 2 to 3½–4 minutes.

FROM THE TOP: Lemon soufflé; Plum and apple fool

CINNAMON BAKED PEARS

4 firm dessert pears, halved and cored
6 tablespoons orange juice
6 tablespoons water
½ teaspoon ground cinnamon
25 g (1 oz) raisins
grated rind of 1 small orange
2 teaspoons cornflour
soured cream or plain unsweetened yogurt,
  to serve

Power setting: Full/Maximum
Preparation and cooking time: 15 minutes, plus standing

1. Place the pears in a shallow serving dish, cut sides up and with the narrow ends to the centre of the dish.
2. Place the orange juice, water, cinnamon, raisins, orange rind and cornflour in a jug, blending well. Cook for 2–2½ minutes until thickened, stirring twice.
3. Spoon over the pears, cover and cook for 4–6 minutes until just tender, rearranging them and basting them with the sauce twice. Leave to stand, covered, for 5 minutes before serving.
4. Serve warm or cold topped with a little soured cream or yogurt.

COMBINATION OVENS:
Prepare and cook as above using *microwave only* but increase the cooking times in Step 2 to 2½–3 minutes and in Step 3 to 4½–7 minutes.

SPONGE CASTLES WITH HOT CHERRY SAUCE

SERVES 8
100 g (4 oz) plain flour
150 g (5 oz) caster sugar
1¼ teaspoons baking powder
½ teaspoon salt
½ teaspoon vanilla essence
65 g (2½ oz) margarine
2 eggs
85 ml (3 fl oz) milk
2 teaspoons grated lemon rind

Cherry sauce:
1 x 425 g (15 oz) can stoned black or red
  cherries
2–3 teaspoons arrowroot powder
1½ teaspoons lemon juice

To decorate:
julienne strips of lemon rind
sprigs of mint

Power setting: Full/Maximum
Preparation and cooking time: 15 minutes

1. Mix the flour with the sugar, baking powder, salt, vanilla essence, margarine, eggs, milk and the lemon rind, beating well until smooth and well mixed.
2. Spoon the mixture into 8 paper drink cups and arrange them in a ring on a plate or on the base of the microwave. Cook for 3–4½ minutes, or until the are almost dry on top, rotating the cups every 1 minute. allow to stand for 1 minute, then carefully loosen the edges with a small spatula and turn out the castles on to a serving plate.
3. Drain the juice from the cherries into a bowl. Add the arrowroot and lemon juice, blending well. Cook for 2–3 minutes until smooth and thickened, stirring twice. Add the cherries and cook for 30 seconds.
4. Spoon a little of the sauce over the sponge castles and decorate with lemon julienne strips and sprigs of mint. Serve the remaining sauce separately and hand plain unsweetened yogurt as well, if liked.

FREEZING DETAILS
1. Prepare the recipe to the end of Step 2.
2. Cool quickly, cover, seal, label and freeze for up to 1 month.

REHEATING DETAILS
Power setting: Full/Maximum
Defrosting and reheating time: 3½–4¾ minutes
1. Remove all wrappings. Place the sponge castles on a plate. Cook for 1–1¼ minutes then leave to stand for 5–10 minutes.
2. Proceed from Step 3 above.

COMBINATION OVENS:
Prepare and cook as above using *microwave only* but increase the cooking times in Step 2 to 3½–5½ minutes and Step 3 to 2½–3½ minutes.
Reheating details: Follow the instructions above using *microwave only* but increase the cooking time in Step 1 to 1¼ to 1½ minutes.

FROM THE TOP: Cinnamon baked pears; Sponge castles with hot cherry sauce

PEPPERMINT MERINGUE WITH PEARS

SERVES 6
275 g (10 oz) icing sugar, sifted
1 egg white, lightly beaten
1 teaspoon peppermint essence
6 canned pear halves, well drained
300 ml (½ pint) double cream
50 g (2 oz) plain chocolate
toasted flaked almonds, to decorate
 (optional)

Power setting: Full/Maximum and Medium
Preparation and cooking time: about 30 minutes, plus cooling

This is the nearest microwave equivalent to a traditional meringue – the microwave version is, however, much crisper and far sweeter so serving sizes should be small.
1. Mix the icing sugar with the egg white and peppermint essence to form a soft dough. Knead lightly until smooth and shiny.
2. Pat the dough into a 15 cm (6 inch) circle and place on a round serving dish. Cook on medium power for 5 minutes, then increase the power setting to full/maximum and cook for a further 1 minute until firm and crisp. Leave to cool.
3. When cool, top the meringue with the pear halves. Whip the cream until it stands in soft peaks and pipe or swirl decoratively over the meringue and pears.
4. Place the chocolate in a bowl and cook on medium power for 2–2½ minutes, stirring once, until melted. Drizzle over the pear and cream mixture. Decorate with toasted almonds, if wished, and serve

lightly chilled. Ideally serve within 1–2 hours of topping with the pear, cream and chocolate.

COMBINATION OVENS:
Prepare and cook as above using *microwave only* but increase the cooking times in Step 2 on medium power to 6 minutes then on full/maximum power to 1–1¼ minutes and Step 4 on medium power to 2½–3 minutes.

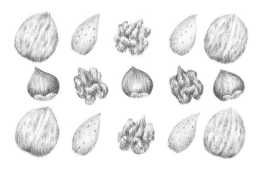

CRÈME CARAMEL

3 tablespoons sugar
3 tablespoons water
350 ml (12 fl oz) milk
1 tablespoon vanilla sugar
2 eggs, lightly beaten

Power setting: Full/Maximum and Low
Preparation and cooking time: about 30 minutes, plus cooling and chilling

1. Place the sugar and 1 tablespoon of the water in a 600 ml (1 pint) heatproof soufflé dish. Cook on full/maximum power for 3 minutes until the mixture is pale brown.
2. Add the remaining water and cook on full/maximum power for 4–4½ minutes until the mixture is caramelized and a rich golden colour. Allow to cool slightly while preparing the custard mixture.
3. Place the milk and vanilla sugar in a jug and cook on full/maximum power for 2 minutes, stirring once. Pour over the eggs, blending well. Strain over the caramel mixture.
4. Cover loosely and cook on low power for 8–10 minutes until lightly set and just firm to the touch. Leave to stand, covered, for 10 minutes.

5. Serve warm straight from the dish or allow to cool, then chill for 2 hours. Invert on to a serving dish to serve lightly chilled with cream, if liked.

COMBINATION OVENS:
Prepare and cook as above using *microwave only* but increase the cooking times in Step 1 on full/maximum power to 3½ minutes; Step 2 on full/maximum power to 4½–5 minutes; Step 3 on full/maximum power to 2½ minutes and Step 4 on low power for 9–12 minutes.

FROM THE TOP: Peppermint meringue with pears; Crème caramel

RHUBARB AND GINGER CRUMBLE

750 g (1½ lb) rhubarb, chopped
1 small cooking apple, peeled, cored and
  chopped
1 teaspoon ground ginger
50 g (2 oz) brown sugar
25 g (1 oz) crystallized or preserved ginger,
  chopped

Topping:
75 g (3 oz) butter
175 g (6 oz) wholemeal flour
50 g (2 oz) demerara sugar

Power setting: Full/Maximum
Preparation and cooking time: about
25 minutes

1. Mix the rhubarb with the apple, ginger, sugar and crystallized or preserved ginger in a flameproof pie or pudding dish.
2. To make the topping, rub the butter into the flour until the mixture resembles fine breadcrumbs. Stir in the sugar, blending well. Carefully spoon over the top of the fruit.
3. Cook for 11–13 minutes, giving the dish a quarter turn every 3 minutes. Brown under a preheated hot grill, if liked, before serving. Serve with custard, cream, ice cream or yogurt.

COMBINATION OVENS:
Prepare and cook as above to the end of Step 2 then *comination bake* at 200°C using *low* power for 20 minutes.

Fruit crumbles are delicious puddings, loved by young and old alike. For an interesting variation on the traditional crumble topping, try replacing 40 g (1½ oz) of the flour with a rich fruit and nut muesli mixture. However, if you use a very sweet muesli, remember to cut down on the sugar otherwise the dish will be too sweet.

FRUIT KISSEL

750 g (1½ lb) mixed berry fruits, e.g.
  raspberries, strawberries, blackcurrants,
  redcurrants and blackberries
150 ml (¼ pint) orange or apple juice
100 ml (3½ fl oz) water
4 tablespoons clear honey
4 teaspoons arrowroot powder
plain unsweetened yogurt, to decorate
  (optional)
crisp dessert biscuits, to serve

Power setting: Full/Maximum
Preparation and cooking time: 10–15
minutes, plus chilling

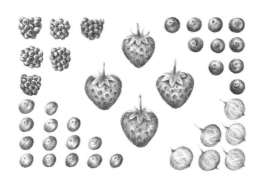

1. Place the berry fruits in a large bowl. Mix the orange or apple juice with the water, clear honey and arrowroot, blending well.
2. Pour the juice mixture over the fruit, cover and cook for 4–5 minutes, stirring every 1 minute, until the mixture is clear and lightly thickened.
3. Stir gently to blend. Top with a swirl of yogurt, if liked, and serve with a selection of crisp dessert biscuits.

COMBINATION OVENS:
Prepare and cook as above using *microwave only* but increase the cooking time in Step 2 to 4½–6 minutes.

FROM THE TOP: Rhubarb and ginger crumble; Fruit kissel

BREAD, CAKES AND BISCUITS

You no longer have to set aside a day, or even half a day to make a baker's dozen microwave breads, biscuits and cakes. A whole host of teatime treats and staples can now be speedily cooked in the microwave. Choose from yeast-baked specialities like Chelsea buns, traditional wholemeal bread and rich fruit cake, moist melted mixtures like gingerbread and a wicked, but really supreme, chocolate cake.

Florentines (recipe, page 118)

SCONES

MAKES 8–10
225 g (8 oz) plain flour
1 tablespoon baking powder
pinch of salt
50 g (2 oz) butter
1 tablespoon caster sugar
150 ml (¼ pint) milk
oil to brush the browning dish

Power setting: Full/Maximum
Preparation and cooking time: about 15 minutes, plus cooling

1. Sift the flour, baking powder and salt into a bowl. Rub in the butter until the mixture resembles fine breadcrumbs and stir in the sugar. Bind to a soft but not sticky dough with the milk.
2. Roll out the dough on a lightly floured surface to about 4 cm (1½ inches) thick and cut out 8–10 rounds using a 5 cm (2 inch) cutter.
3. Preheat a large browning dish for 5 minutes (or according to the manufacturer's instructions). Lightly brush the base with oil.
4. Add the scones, pressing down well and cook for 1 minute. Turn over with a spatula and cook for a further 1½–2 minutes.
5. Transfer to a wire rack to cool. Serve warm or cold, split and buttered.

COMBINATION OVENS:
Prepare and cook as above using *microwave only* but increase the cooking times in Step 4 to 1¼, then 1¾–2¼ minutes or cook by *convection only* on a baking tray at 220°C for 12 minutes (the tops may be glazed with a little milk before cooking, if liked).

BASIC WHITE BREAD

MAKES 1 LARGE 1 KG (2 LB) LOAF
    OR 3 SMALL LOAVES
750 g (1½ lb) strong plain white flour
1 teaspoon salt
50 g (2 oz) butter or margarine
1 sachet easy-blend dried yeast
400 ml (14 fl oz) warm water or water and milk mixed
beaten egg, to glaze
kibbled wheat, to sprinkle (optional)

Power setting: Full/Maximum
Preparation and cooking time: about 30 minutes, plus proving

1. Sift the flour and salt into a bowl. Rub in the butter and stir in the yeast. Add the liquid and mix to a smooth dough. Turn out on to a lightly floured surface and knead until smooth and elastic, about 5–10 minutes. Place in an oiled bowl and leave to rise until double in size.
2. Turn out the dough on to a lightly floured surface, knock back to release all the air bubbles and knead again for 5 minutes. Shape the dough to fit a large 1 kg (2 lb) greased loaf dish or large round greased soufflé dish or divide and shape to fit 3 small greased loaf dishes. Place in the dishes, cover with cling film and leave to rise until double in size. Brush with a little beaten egg to glaze and sprinkle with kibbled wheat, if liked.
3. Cook for 5½–7 minutes, giving the dish or dishes a quarter turn every 2 minutes until cooked. Allow to cool on a wire rack. The loaves can be quickly browned and crisped under a preheated hot conventional grill for a few minutes until golden after cooking.

COMBINATION OVENS:
Prepare as above to the end of Step 2 (better results are often achieved in combination ovens if the dough is divided into three loaves for cooking). *Combination bake* at 220° C using *low* power for 15–20 minutes, or until well risen, golden and cooked. When cooked the loaves should sound hollow when rapped on the bottom with the knuckles. Allow to cool on a wire rack.

FROM THE LEFT: Scones; Basic white bread

WHOLEMEAL LOAF

MAKES 1 LARGE 1 kg (2 lb) LOAF
   OR 3 SMALL LOAVES
750 g (1½ lb) plain wholemeal flour or
   350 g (12 oz) plain wholemeal and 350 g
   (12 oz) granary flour
1 teaspoon salt
25 g (1 oz) butter
25 g (1 oz) lard
1 sachet easy-blend dried yeast
400 ml (14 fl oz) warm water or water and
   milk mixed
kibbled wheat or bran, to sprinkle

Power setting: Full/Maximum
Preparation and cooking time: about 1
hour

1. Sift the flours and salt into a bowl, adding any bran left in the sieve. Rub in the fats and stir in the yeast. Add the liquid and mix to a smooth dough. Turn on to a lightly floured surface and knead until smooth and elastic, about 5–10 minutes. Place in an oiled bowl and leave to rise until doubled in size.
2. Turn the dough on to a lightly floured surface, knock back to release all the air bubbles and knead again for about 5 minutes. Shape the dough to fit a large 1 kg (2 lb) greased loaf dish or large round greased soufflé dish or divide and shape to fit three small greased loaf dishes. Place in the dishes, cover with cling film and leave to rise until doubled in size. Brush with a little water or milk and sprinkle with kibbled wheat or bran.
3. Cook for 5½–7 minutes, giving the dish or dishes a quarter–turn every 2 minutes

until cooked. Allow to cool on a wire rack. The loaves can be quickly browned and crisped under a preheated hot conventional grill for a few minutes after cooking.

COMBINATION OVENS:
Prepare as above to the end of Step 2 (better results are often achieved in combination ovens if the dough is divided into three loaves for cooking). *Combination bake* at 220° C using *low* power for 15–20 minutes, or until well–risen, golden and cooked. When cooked the loaves should sound hollow when rapped on the bottom with the knuckles. Allow to cool on a wire rack.

CHEESY SODA BREAD

MAKES 1 LARGE LOAF
450 g (1 lb) plain white or wholemeal flour
2 tablespoons mustard powder
2 teaspoons bicarbonate of soda
2 teaspoons cream of tartar
1 teaspoon salt
25 g (1 oz) lard
1 teaspoon dried sage
100 g (4 oz) Cheddar cheese, grated
300 ml (½ pint) milk
1 tablespoon lemon juice
25 g (1 oz) porridge oats

Power setting: Medium and Full/
Maximum
Preparation and cooking time: about
20–25 minutes, plus cooling

1. Mix the flour with the mustard powder, bicarbonate of soda, cream of tartar and salt.
2. Rub in the lard until the mixture resembles fine breadcrumbs. Stir in the sage and cheese, blending well.
3. Mix the milk with the lemon juice and mix into the dry ingredients, blending well to make a soft dough. Knead on a lightly floured surface until smooth and elastic then shape into a round and sprinkle with the oats.
4. Place on a large plate and mark into 4 sections with a sharp knife to make a cross. Cook on medium power for 5 minutes, giving the plate a half-turn once.
5. Increase the power setting to full/maximum and cook for a further 3 minutes. Leave to stand for 10 minutes before transferring to a wire rack to cool.

COMBINATION OVENS:
(Makes 2 small loaves). Prepare as above to the end of Step 2. Mix the milk with the lemon juice and mix into the dry ingredients, blending well to make a soft dough. Knead on a lightly floured surface until smooth and elastic. Divide into two equal pieces and shape each into a neat round and sprinkle with the oats. Cook one at a time, place on a ovenproof plate and mark into 4 sections with a sharp knife to make a cross. *Combination bake* at 180°C using *medium* power for 10 minutes, or until the bread is well risen and browned. Repeat with the remaining loaf. Transfer to a wire rack to cool.

FROM THE TOP: Wholemeal loaf; Cheesy soda bread

FLAPJACKS

MAKES ABOUT 16 PIECES
100 g (4 oz) butter
25 g (1 oz) caster sugar
40 g (1½ oz) soft brown sugar
4 tablespoons golden syrup
pinch of salt
200 g (7 oz) rolled oats
50 g (2 oz) grapenuts

Power setting: Full/Maximum
Preparation and cooking time: 15
minutes, plus cooling

1. Lightly grease a 23 cm (9 inch) square shallow glass dish.
2. Place the butter and sugars in a bowl and cook for 1½ minutes.
3. Mix in the golden syrup, salt, oats and grapenuts, blending well to mix thoroughly. Press the mixture evenly into the prepared dish and level the surface.
4. Cook for 5 minutes, giving the dish a quarter turn every 1¼ minutes. Leave to cool in the dish. Cut into squares to serve when cold.

COMBINATION OVENS:
Prepare and cook as above using *microwave only* but increase the cooking times in Step 2 to 1¾ minutes and Step 4 to 5¾–6 minutes.

CHELSEA BUNS

MAKES 8
15 g (½ oz) fresh yeast or 1½ teaspoons
  dried yeast
½ teaspoon caster sugar
120 ml (4 fl oz) milk
225 g (8 oz) plain flour
½ teaspoon salt
20 g (¾ oz) butter
1 egg, beaten

Filling:
25 g (1 oz) butter
150 g (5 oz) currants
50 g (2 oz) soft brown sugar
soft brown sugar for sprinkling
pinch of ground cinnamon
2 tablespoons sieved apricot jam or honey

Power setting: Full/Maximum
Preparation and cooking time: about
50 minutes

FROM THE LEFT: Chelsea buns; Flapjacks

1. Lightly grease a large shallow 18 cm (7 inch) round dish and line the base with greaseproof paper.
2. Place the yeast in a small bowl with the sugar. Place the milk in a small bowl and cook for 30 seconds until warm. Pour on to the yeast and sugar and mix well. Leave until frothy, about 10–15 minutes.
3. Sift the flour and salt into a bowl and rub in the butter. Add the yeast mixture and egg and beat to make a soft dough. Knead until smooth and elastic, cover and leave in a warm place until doubled in size.
4. Knock back the dough and roll out to a rectangle measuring 30 x 23 cm (12 x 9 inches).
5. To make the filling, place the butter in a bowl and cook for 1 minute to melt. Brush over the dough and sprinkle with the currants and sugar. Roll up from one of the long ends like a Swiss roll.
6. Cut across the roll to make 8 slices and place, cut side down, in the prepared cooking dish. Cover and leave in a warm place until doubled in size.
7. Sprinkle the top with a little extra sugar and cinnamon and cook for 4–5 minutes, giving the dish a half-turn once. Leave to stand for 5–10 minutes before cooling the

Chelsea buns on a wire rack.
8. Place the jam or honey in a bowl and cook for ½ minute to soften. Brush over the Chelsea buns while still hot to glaze.

COMBINATION OVENS:
Prepare and cook as above using *microwave only* to the end of Step 6. Sprinkle the top with a little extra sugar and cinnamon and *combination bake* at 200°C using *low* power for 14–18 minutes, until golden brown and cooked. Glaze as above in Step 8, if liked.

VICTORIA SANDWICH

MAKES 1 x 20 CM (8 INCH) ROUND
  CAKE
175 g (6 oz) butter
175 g (6 oz) caster sugar
3 eggs, beaten
175 g (6 oz) self-raising flour, sifted
2 tablespoons hot water or milk
3–4 tablespoons raspberry jam
sifted icing sugar, to dust
fresh strawberries or raspberries, to
  decorate

Power setting: Full/Maximum
Preparation and cooking time: about
20 minutes, plus cooling

1. Grease and line the base of a 20 cm (8 inch) deep round cake dish or soufflé dish with greaseproof paper.
2. Cream the butter and sugar until light and fluffy. Add the eggs a little at a time with a tablespoon of the flour. Carefully fold in the remaining flour with the water or milk.
3. Spoon into the cake dish and smooth the surface. Cook for 6½–7½ minutes, giving the dish a quarter turn every 1½–2 minutes. The cake will still be slightly sticky and moist on the surface when cooked but will dry out after standing for 5 minutes. Turn out to cool on a wire rack.
4. When cool cut the cake in half and sandwich together with the jam. Dust the top with icing sugar and decorate with fresh strawberries or raspberries.

COMBINATION OVENS:
Prepare and cook as above to the end of Step 2. Spoon into the cake dish and smooth the surface, making a small hollow in the centre of the mixture. *Combination bake* at 200°C using *low* power for 15 minutes, or until browned and the top springs back when lightly touched with the fingertips. Leave to stand in the dish for 5–10 minutes before turning out to cool on a wire rack. Proceed as in Step 4 above.

FLORENTINES

MAKES 12–15
50 g (2 oz) butter
50 g (2 oz) demerara sugar
1 tablespoon golden syrup
50 g (2 oz) glacé cherries, chopped
75 g (3 oz) walnuts, chopped
25 g (1 oz) sultanas
25 g (1 oz) blanched almonds, chopped
25 g (1 oz) cut mixed peel
25 g (1 oz) plain flour
about 100 g (4 oz) plain chocolate
  (optional)

Power setting: Full/Maximum and
Medium
Preparation and cooking time: about
20 minutes, plus cooling

1. Place the butter, sugar and golden syrup in a bowl. Cook on full/maximum power for 1–1½ minutes until melted.
2. Add the cherries, walnuts, sultanas, almonds, mixed peel and flour and mix well to blend.
3. Cook the florentines in about 3 batches by placing teaspoonfuls of the mixture, spaced well apart, on greaseproof paper. Cook each batch on full/maximum power for about 1½ minutes. Remove from the oven and shape the edges neatly with the side of a fork.
4. When slightly cooled and firm, lift carefully with a palette knife on to a cooling rack. Serve plain or coat one side with melted chocolate, if liked. To coat with chocolate, break the chocolate into a bowl and cook on medium power for 2½–3 minutes, stirring twice. Spread over one side of the florentines and leave to cool and set.

COMBINATION OVENS:
Prepare and cook as above using *microwave only* but increase the cooking time in Step 1 on full/maximum power to 1½–1¾ minutes; Step 3 on full/maximum power to 1¾ minutes and Step 4 on medium power to 3–3½ minutes.

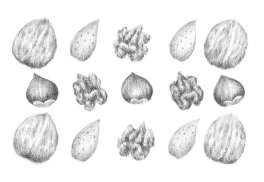

FROM THE TOP: Victoria sandwich; Florentines

SUPREME CHOCOLATE CAKE

MAKES 1 x 18–20 CM (7–8 INCH) CAKE

50 g (2 oz) flaked almonds
175 g (6 oz) butter, softened
175 g (6 oz) dark brown sugar
3 large eggs (sizes 1 or 2)
5 tablespoons clear honey
150 ml (¼ pint) soured cream
175 g (6 oz) self-raising flour
6 tablespoons cocoa powder
6 tablespoons ground almonds
3 tablespoons granulated sugar
3 tablespoons cold water

Sauce:
40 g (1½ oz) butter
175 g (6 oz) plain chocolate
6 tablespoons brown rum

Power setting: Full/Maximum
Preparation and cooking time: about 40 minutes, plus cooling

1. Grease and line the base of a 2 litre (3½ pint) deep round straight–sided casserole or soufflé dish with greaseproof paper.
2. Arrange the flaked almonds in a single layer on a plate. Cook for 5 minutes, stirring twice, until golden, checking frequently. Allow to cool on absorbent paper towels.
3. Cream the butter and brown sugar until pale and fluffy. Beat in the eggs, one at a time, then the honey and soured cream. Sift the flour and cocoa together. Fold lightly into the cake mixture with a metal spoon. Finally fold in the ground almonds.
4. Spoon the mixture into the prepared dish and cook for 10 minutes, giving the dish a quarter turn every 2½ minutes, until cooked. Sprinkle at once with the toasted flaked almonds.
5. Place the sugar and water in a small bowl and cook for 3–4 minutes until just beginning to caramelize. Very quickly drizzle over the flaked almonds on the cake surface. Leave to stand for 10 minutes then invert on to a baking sheet, then on to a wire rack to cool.
6. The cake may be served plain at this stage or with the chocolate rum sauce. To make the sauce, place the butter and chocolate in a bowl. Cook for 3 minutes, stirring twice, until melted. Whisk in the rum and serve at once. This sauce hardens quickly on cooling but can be melted again using defrost power for 1–2 minutes.

COMBINATION OVENS:
Prepare and cook as above using *microwave only* but increase the cooking times in Step 2 to 6 minutes; Step 4 to 11½ minutes; Step 5 to 3½–4½ minutes and Step 6 to 3½ minutes.

RICH FRUIT CAKE

MAKES 1 x 15 CM (6 INCH) ROUND CAKE

150 g (5 oz) butter
150 g (5 oz) brown sugar
grated rind of ½ lemon
3 eggs, beaten
175 g (6 oz) plain flour
¼ teaspoon ground mixed spice
¼ teaspoon ground cinnamon
450 g (1 lb) mixed dried fruit
50 g (2 oz) glacé cherries, halved
25 g (1 oz) chopped nuts
1 tablespoon black treacle
1 tablespoon brandy

Power setting: Defrost
Preparation and cooking time: about 1¼–1½ hours

1. Cream the butter with the sugar until light and fluffy. Beat in the lemon rind and eggs, a little at a time, until well blended.
2. Sift the flour with the spice and cinnamon and fold into the creamed mixture.
3. Fold in the mixed fruit, glacé cherries, nuts, treacle and brandy, mixing well.
4. Spoon into a greased and greaseproof paper lined 15 cm (6 inch) deep round cake or soufflé dish and make a slight hollow in the centre to enable the cake to rise evenly.
5. Cook for 35–40 minutes, giving the dish a quarter turn every 8 minutes. The cake is cooked when a skewer inserted into the centre of the cake comes out clean. Allow to cool slightly, then turn out on to a wire rack to cool completely. Store for 1 month in an airtight tin to allow the flavours to mature.

COMBINATION OVENS:
Prepare as above to the end of Step 4. *Combination bake* at 140°C using *low* power for 55–65 minutes or until a skewer inserted into the centre of the cake comes out clean. Cool and store as above.

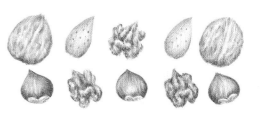

FROM THE TOP: Supreme chocolate cake; Rich fruit cake

CARAWAY SEED CAKE

MAKES 1 x 18 CM (7 INCH) ROUND CAKE

175 g (6 oz) butter
175 g (6 oz) caster sugar
3 eggs, beaten
225 g (8 oz) plain flour
1½ teaspoons baking powder
2 tablespoons milk
3 teaspoons caraway seeds
ground mixed spice or cinnamon, to
* sprinkle (optional)*

Power setting: Medium and Full/Maximum
Preparation and cooking time: about 20 minutes, plus cooling

1. Lightly grease the base and sides of an 18 cm (7 inch) deep round cake or straight-sided soufflé dish. Line the base with a disc of greaseproof paper.
2. Cream the butter with the sugar until light and fluffy. Beat in the eggs with a little of the flour if the mixture starts to curdle. Sift the remaining flour with the baking powder and fold into the creamed mixture with the milk. Finally fold in the caraway seeds.
3. Spoon into the prepared cake dish and level the surface. Sprinkle with a little ground mixed spice or cinnamon, if liked. Bake at medium power for 10 minutes, giving the dish a quarter-turn every 2½ minutes to ensure it rises evenly. Increase the power to full/maximum and cook for 1 minute until the cake is well-risen and firm to the touch – test by inserting a skewer into the centre of the cake; it is cooked if the skewer comes out clean. Allow to cool in the dish for a few minutes then turn out on to a wire rack to cool.
4. The cake can be quickly browned under a preheated hot conventional grill after cooking to give a traditional browned crust.

COMBINATION OVENS:
Prepare as in Steps 1 and 2 above. Spoon into the prepared cake dish and level the surface. *Combination bake at 200°C using low power for 14 minutes or until well-risen, golden and the top springs back lightly when touched with the fingertips. Allow to cool in the dish before transferring to a wire rack.*

WALNUT CAKE

MAKES 1 x 1 KG (2 LB) LOAF

175 g (6 oz) butter or margarine
175 g (6 oz) soft brown sugar
3 eggs, beaten
225 g (8 oz) plain flour
1½ teaspoons baking powder
½ teaspoon salt
2 tablespoons milk
1 teaspoon vanilla essence
75 g (3 oz) chopped walnuts

Power setting: Medium
Preparation and cooking time: about 20 minutes, plus cooling

1. Line a 1 kg (2 lb) loaf dish with greaseproof paper, then grease again.
2. Cream the butter or margarine and the sugar until light and fluffy. Add the eggs, a little at a time, beating well to blend.
3. Sift the flour with the baking powder and salt. Fold into the creamed mixture with the milk and vanilla essence, using a metal spoon. Finally fold in the walnuts.
4. Spoon into the prepared loaf dish and level the surface. Shield the ends of the loaf dish with 5 cm (2 inch) strips of foil. Stand on an upturned saucer in the microwave and cook for 11–13 minutes, removing the foil strips after 6 minutes, until well-risen and firm to the touch, giving the dish a quarter turn every 3 minutes. Leave to stand for 5 minutes before turning out on to a wire rack to cool.

COMBINATION OVENS:
Prepare as above to the end of Step 3. Spoon into the prepared loaf dish and *combination bake at 220°C using medium power for 12–14 minutes, or until it is well risen, browned and springy to the touch.* Test by inserting a wooden cocktail stick into the centre of the cake – if it comes out clean of mixture the cake is cooked. Leave to stand for 5 minutes before turning out to cool on a wire rack.

FROM THE TOP: Caraway seed cake; Walnut cake

RECIPE AND MENU PLANNER

DINNER PARTY DISHES

Monkfish Appetizer: page 14

Fresh Asparagus with Herbed Butter Sauce: page 25

Rack of Lamb with Walnut Stuffing: page 44

Peking Duck: page 57

Peppermint Meringue with Pears: page 107

BUFFET AND OUTDOOR ENTERTAINING

Bagna Cauda: page 16

Mini Meatballs with Spicy Dip: page 9

Picnic Loin of Pork with Mustard Sauce: page 50

Fruity Potato Salad: page 25

Lemon Soufflé: page 102

SPECIALLY FOR CHILDREN

Sausage Brioches: page 52

Jacket Potatoes: page 134

Flapjacks: page 117

Pasta Quills with Cheese and Bacon: page 90

Chelsea Buns: page 117

Sponge Castles with Cherry Sauce: page 104

VEGETARIAN MEALS

Creamy Carrot Soup with Croûtons: page 12

Cheesy Stuffed Mushrooms: page 22

Tomato and Courgette Quiche: page 32

Spiced Chick Peas with Fruit and Vegetables: page 94

Tortellini in Creamy Pesto Sauce: page 96

Blackcurrant Baked Cheesecake: page 100

FAMILY MEALS

Rabbit Hotpot with Caraway Dumplings: page 56

Gammon Steaks with Orange and Honey: page 43

Beef and Kidney Horseradish Stew: page 43

Devonshire Cod: page 78

Green Beans in Tangy Tomato Sauce: page 20

Autumn Bramble Pudding: page 100

$\mathscr{F}$OOD FACTS

HELEN DORE

THE BENEFITS OF MICROWAVE COOKING

The microwave method is the most exciting development ever in the modern kitchen and has revolutionized our approach to cooking. Here are 20 reasons why.

- Sensationally short cooking times make the microwave the ultimate time-saver. A jacket potato cooks in 4-5 minutes and a steamed pudding in 7-9 minutes.
- The microwave method is so modern. It offers the busy cook unprecedented flexibility and spontaneity in meal-planning.
- The microwave cooker is multi-functional. It can steam, poach, boil, bake, roast, even achieve a grilled effect, and may be used to even further advantage in combination with a conventional oven and freezer.
- A great variety of containers can be used for microwave cooking and serving, which means minimal washing up, with no pans to scour.
- A wide range of specially developed microware, as well as increasingly sophisticated features in the cookers themselves, create special effects such as browning, which original microwave models were unable to do.
- Because the microwave cooker

interior stays cool during cooking, there are no burnt-on spillages to remove.
- The microwave oven is super-easy to clean – a wipe-down with a soapy cloth is all that is needed.
- As microwave cooking requires little liquid it preserves excellent flavour and texture, especially in soft foods like fish, and original colours, particularly with green vegetables.
- Microwave cooking is specially healthy, because it retains all the valuable nutrients in food, and little added fat is needed.
- Food can be reheated and thawed in the microwave cooker in a fraction of the time required with a conventional oven, without loss of flavour, texture or quality.
- Easy reheating makes the

microwave ideal for families requiring meals at different times.
- It's also perfect for small families – couples out at work all day, or people living on their own.
- Microwave cookers are super-safe. Manufacturers' tests are stringent, the power switches off automatically when the oven door opens, and there is no danger of burning, as with other cooking methods. This makes the microwave ideal for the elderly and the disabled to use.
- The microwave cooker is so easy to operate that children can safely use it. In fact it's a great way to encourage children to learn to cook.
- There's a wide variety of microwave models to choose from to suit individual needs, either counter-top, wall-mounted as part of a fitted kitchen, or as part of a combination oven.
- Whatever the model chosen, it will take up little space, making it ideal for even the smallest kitchen.
- A microwave cooker creates minimal cooking odours, making it perfect for an open-plan kitchen.
- There is no condensation with a microwave cooker, as there can be with a hob, and the kitchen stays pleasantly cool.
- The microwave cooker need not be confined to the kitchen – it can be used instead of a hostess trolley in the dining room, or in a family room, studio or student's room. It can even be transported to a holiday cottage.
- Best of all, microwave cooking is so economical. Short cooking times save energy and money: there's no fuel-wasting pre-heating or cooling down. Most microwave cookers run off a 13 amp socket outlet and cost only a few pence per hour to run on full power.

WHAT ARE MICROWAVES?

When the microwave cooker is switched on, the electric current is transformed from high-directional to indirectional voltage and converted into microwaves by means of a fuse called a magnetron located inside the cooker.

Microwaves are electro-magnetic, high-frequency, short-length waves, similar to the waves used to transmit a television picture, radio sound or radar systems. Unlike X-rays, for example,

they are non-ionizing and cannot build up within the body or damage the cell structure.

Microwaves are deflected by metal. As they enter the cooker, they bounce off the metal walls and are distributed evenly around the oven cavity by means of a wave guide or stirrer fan set in the side or the roof, or by a turntable. Microwaves can only be produced when the cooker door is shut and the timer on.

HOW THE MICROWAVES COOK FOOD

Microwaves are attracted to moisture, causing the water molecules in food to vibrate at an incredible 2,000 million times per second, thus generating intense heat within the food. This is the key to the microwave cooking method – the food cooks from within, not by means of an external source of heat as with conventional cooking. In fact, microwaves penetrate the surface of food to a depth of only about 5 cm (2 inches):

the centre of a large piece of food such as a joint of meat, for example, cooks by conduction of the heat produced near the surface. Food cooked by the microwave method continues to cook after the energy is switched off, due to heat conduction. This is why 'standing time' is often specified in microwave recipes.

As microwaves deflect off metal they will not cook food in a metal container.

In fact metal will damage the magnetron, and the only form of metal which should be allowed inside the microwave oven is tiny pieces of kitchen foil used to protect parts of food from over-cooking. Microwaves will, however, pass through non-metallic materials such as ceramics, glass, paper, wood and plastic, and it is from these that the containers used in microwave cooking are made.

The tube on the right is the magnetron which produces the microwaves

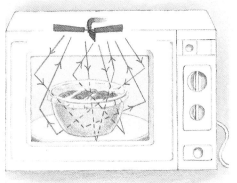

Here, a stirrer fan set in the roof helps distribute microwaves evenly

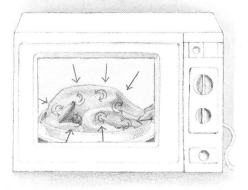

The microwaves make the water molecules in food vibrate, generating the cooking heat

MICROWAVE POWER

Microwave power output is measured in watts and the higher the wattage, the faster the rate of cooking. Most microwave cookers are now 700, 650 or 600 watts: some older models may be only 500 or 400 watts.

Power output and heat controls are not standardized in microwave cookers as they are in conventional ovens. There are a number of microwave control settings, which vary according to model.
Cook control switch: this activates the microwave energy and is switched off when the cooker door is opened. For

cooking to resume, the door must be closed again.
Timer: this may be mechanical or digital and is measured in minutes/ seconds. When the pre-set cooking time is reached, the power is automatically turned off and a buzzer will sound.
Variable power setting: this may be dial, digital press button or touch control type, and may be expressed as HIGH/ MEDIUM/LOW; in percentages, e.g. 100%, 60%, 35%; or, in terms of cooking methods, e.g. ROAST, SIMMER, REHEAT.

Automatic programmer: this is pre-set to enable food to cook at different power settings by means of a memory bank, without manual adjustment.
Defrost control is designed to thaw frozen food fast and is specially useful for thawing large items of food. Once the control is set the microwave energy is reduced, to avoid cooking the food.

All microwave ovens can operate only when the door, which has a special seal and locking system and may be sideways-opening, drop-down or slide-up, is completely shut – an invaluable safety precaution.

Double oven: Several microwave ovens are available incorporated into the conventional oven set-up. In most cases, the microwave acts as the second oven but is still separate from the conventional oven.

Most models of portable and double ovens are electric, but a model combining conventional gas cooking and electric microwave cooking has recently become available. It is not portable.

Good ventilation is essential to allow moisture to escape from the microwave oven during cooking. Cookers fitted with vents at the top should not be sited beneath a cupboard or shelf, and those with vents at the back should not be placed against a wall. Some models have special filters to circulate air through the oven.

COMBINATION MICROWAVE COOKERS

A combination microwave cooker represents kitchen technology at the highest level. It means you can cook by both microwave and conventional methods in the same oven, combining the advantages of both simultaneously, or using each method separately, if required. For example a combination oven will cook microwave-fast in a fraction of the time taken by the conventional method, but it will also crisp and brown food in a way that does not come naturally to the microwave-only method. It really does offer the best of both worlds.

Combination microwave models offer:
Microwave facility which may be used alone, like a basic microwave oven, or it can be used in combination with:

Convection cooking – sometimes fan-assisted – in the same way as an ordinary conventional oven;
Halogen heat (in some latest models), with top and side/top only options for overall browning or grilling;
Grill facility (ideal for browning some microwaved dishes);
Hob facility.

A combination microwave oven offers the fullest range of cooking choice in the most compact form within a single model, which may be table-top or built-in. It is the ideal choice for smaller kitchens where there would not be space for a full-sized separate cooker as well as a microwave cooker and ideal for cottages and other holiday accommodation.

SPECIAL MICROWAVE COOKER FEATURES

New microwave cookers offer more and more refinements all the time. Here are some special features to look for.

Removable floor: this special ceramic glass tray can be easily pulled out and washed. It makes dealing with spillages specially easy.

Turntable: food left in one position in the microwave cooker will cook unevenly. An automatically revolving turntable does away with the need to turn or rotate dishes manually during cooking. The turntable can usually be easily removed for cleaning, and to facilitate the cooking of large items such as turkey, which would be too big to rotate.

Stirrer blades, paddles or fans set in the roof of the cooker help distribute the microwaves evenly.

Browning element: located in the top of

Some microwaves have a turntable which enables food to be cooked evenly.

the cooker, this works rather like a conventional electric grill to give microwaved food a browned finish.

Temperature probe or food sensor: this is specially useful to ensure large items of food, like joints of meat and whole

poultry cook through. One end of the probe is inserted into the thickest part of the food, the other is plugged into a special socket in the oven wall. The energy is automatically switched off once the desired temperature is reached. In this way the food is cooked by temperature rather than by time, which is otherwise the norm in microwave cooking.

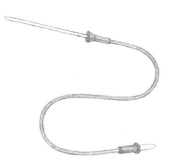

Temperature probes take the guesswork out of cooking joints of meat.

ESSENTIAL COOKING CONTAINERS

Selecting the right containers to hold the food is essential to microwave success. Because microwaves are deflected by metal, cast-iron flameproof casseroles, roasting tins, cake and pie tins, china with metallic decoration and lead crystal cannot be used in microwave cooking; not only will they fail to cook the food, they may also damage the magnetron and cause 'arcing' (sparking) which can pit the oven walls.

Instead, microwave containers must be made of non-metallic, moisture-free materials, such as glass or plastic, which allow the microwaves to pass straight through them. Many of the dishes and containers used in conventional cooking can be used or adapted for the microwave.

Always use the shape and size of the container specified in recipes. On the whole, round, shallow, straight-sided containers give best results with quick, even cooking. Make sure, though, that the container is deep enough to avoid spillage when the food bubbles up, and large enough to hold the food spread out evenly in a single layer. Choosing containers that are suitable to serve from, as well as cook in, means your washing up will be halved.

The following are all suitable for use in the microwave oven:

China and ceramic: glazed china and ceramic dishes, plates, cups, bowls, jugs, etc. are useful microwave containers and even teapots can be used! Avoid unglazed, porous pottery which tends to overheat and slow cooking down. Also avoid antique china and china with a metal trim or pattern.

Glass: heat-resistant glass casseroles, bowls, dishes, plates, jugs, etc. are ideal for microwave use. Ordinary glass tumblers, coupe dishes and small dishes (but not lead crystal or glass with any metal decoration) may also be used, but not to cook food with a high proportion of sugar or fat, as this may cause the glass to overheat and crack. Never leave a thermometer in a bowl when cooking jams or preserves.

Wood and wicker: containers made from these materials, provided they do not contain metal wire or staples or have been bonded with glue, may be used for short cooking times, e.g. for warming bread rolls.

Plastic and paper: special plastic microwave cookware is available, but all plastic containers may be used provided they are dishwasher-proof. Do not use melamine, which can taint food. Thermoplastic containers including boil-in-bags packs and roasting bags are suitable, provided they are pierced to allow steam to escape, and the metal ties replaced with string or elastic bands. Conventional clingfilm designed for wrapping food is best avoided, as the chemicals in the plasticizers it contains may find their way into the food. Instead, use film designed specifically for the microwave. Kitchen paper towels, greaseproof paper and cardboard, providing it does not have a wax finish, are suitable for microwave use. Paper cases are ideal for small cakes.

HOW TO TEST THAT A CONTAINER IS SAFE IN THE MICROWAVE

Place a tumbler half full of water in the container. Cook on Full/Maximum power for 1 minute. If the water is warm and the container remains cool, then the container can safely be used in the microwave.

Heat resistant glass ovenware is ideal as the microwaves can pass through to the food.

ADDITIONAL EQUIPMENT

An increasing range of thermoplastic and glass ceramic containers specially designed for microwave use is now available: vegetable, baking and flan dishes, cake and loaf containers, patty pans and so on. It is worth checking that these are freezerproof: freezer-to-oven-to-tableware, now featured by many manufacturers, is the best possible addition to your own range of microware. The microwave cook will find the following of particular use:

Browning dish: designed to brown and sear food, this comes in a variety of sizes, from single to family servings. A special ceramic glass coating on the dish, designed to absorb microwave energy, is pre-heated in the microwave cooker to a very high temperature. Food such as fish, meat, poultry, onions, etc. is then placed on the hot surface and browns and sears as it would in a frying pan. Browning dishes and skillets specially designed for steaks and other 'grills', stir-fried dishes, and pizzas and other pastry dishes where crispness is required, are invaluable for family microwave cooking. Oven gloves should always be used when handling browning dishes.

Roasting rack: made of special microwave-proof thermoplastic, this deeply grooved dish is designed to raise meat from its juices during cooking, so that it will roast rather than steam or braise. It will also give a crisp, crusty finish to pastry and bread.

Microwave steamer/roaster: this dish with a steaming rack and lid is good for steaming vegetables, fish and puddings, and for roasting small joints.

Microwave baking mould: a deep dish with a hollow centre or centre coil, like a ring mould. This allows microwaves to reach food through the inside as well as the outside, thus speeding up cooking. Ideal for cakes.

Plate rings: these are ideal for stacking and reheating plate meals. Made of plastic, they are placed on plates to enable 2 or 3 to be reheated simultaneously.

Browning dishes work like a conventional frying pan and get very hot

BONUS POINTS

Certain foods and dishes are particularly well suited to microwave cooking, and you will find that you can achieve wonderful results in a fraction of the conventional cooking time.

HERE IS A TOP TEN SELECTION:

- flavourful soups
- succulent fish
- tender meat (especially successful with cheaper cuts), with minimum shrinkage
- egg dishes, especially scrambled and poached eggs
- al dente pasta
- fluffy rice with no sticking
- crisp, colourful vegetables
- steamed puddings
- jams and preserves, especially in small quantities

Plate rings – designed for reheating plate meals for the whole family

MICROWAVE COOKING METHODS

The microwave offers a surprising variety of cooking methods. With all of them, timing is crucial: follow cooking times specified in recipes very precisely. If in doubt, it is best to undercook, check and return the food to the cooker. Food that is over-cooked will dehydrate and harden easily.

Roasting: Microwave-roasted meat shrinks less and retains more of its juices than a conventional roast. With the help of the microwave roasting rack and regular basting during cooking, it is easy to produce a roast with an attractive brown finish. Adding soy sauce, tomato purée, paprika or turmeric gives basting juices extra brownness, which can also be achieved by brushing meat and poultry with redcurrant jelly or honey. Roasting bags, pierced to allow steam to escape, give good results in the microwave.

As compact shapes cook most evenly in the microwave, boned, rolled and carefully tied joints are ideal. Truss poultry securely to help retain the shape. Fat attracts microwaves, so choose meat that is evenly marbled with fat to ensure even cooking. Protect small pieces of bone, as in a rack of lamb or chicken drumsticks, for example, with small pieces of foil overwrapped with microwave film.

Avoid seasoning meat with salt during cooking as this has a toughening effect and always use unsalted butter for cooking meat. Pork rind is the one exception to this rule: it needs to be rubbed with salt if you want crisp crackling. Bacon joints are particularly successful cooked in a combination oven. They can be cooked fast in the microwave, then glazed and crisped in the conventional oven or under the grill.

Pot-roasting and Stewing: less expensive whole joints, such as brisket, and cheaper small cuts of meat can be successfully microwaved this way at medium or low power. Meat and vegetables need to be lightly seared first, either in a browning dish in the microwave oven, or in a frying pan on top of a conventional hob. With the addition of stock and flavourings, the ingredients are then best microwaved in a lidded casserole dish large enough to allow for stirring and turning, or in a pierced roasting bag.

Grilling: Steaks, chops, bacon rashers, sausages, kebabs, hamburgers, fish and poultry pieces can all be cooked in a browning dish or skillet, pre-browning and sealing giving a 'grilled' appearance. Bacon rasher and gammon steaks should be snipped round the fatty edge to prevent curling.

Frying: Deep-frying must never be attempted in the microwave, as the temperature of the oil or fat cannot be controlled properly. However, shallow or stir-frying in a shallow dish may be successfully achieved in the microwave using full power.

Baking: Microwaved sponge cakes rise beautifully, with feather-light results, and fruit cakes are deliciously moist inside, though the outside may harden slightly on cooling. The pale colour of microwave-baked goods may be disguised by the use of chocolate, coffee, treacle, brown sugar, ginger and other spices in cake mixtures, and, of course, by icing the finished cake.

Flapjack-type cookies, as opposed to crisp biscuits, are very successful in the microwave.

Microwaved pastry and bread will not have a naturally crisp crust, as in conventional baking, but wholemeal flour will give extra colour. Rolling it out extra thinly helps to crisp pastry, and pastry cases for flans and tarts should always be baked blind before the filling is added, to avoid sogginess. Shortcrust and suet crust are the most successful microwaved pastries.

Microwave-baked bread will not be crusty, and it's best to bake naturally soft breads like baps in the microwave oven. However, bread rolls will crisp up if popped under a grill or warmed through on a roasting rack.

Boiling: Small quantities of liquid, in small bowls or mugs, for example, will come to the boil remarkably fast.

Steaming and poaching: As microwaves are attracted to the moisture in food, these methods are ideally suited to the microwave cooker, as the food cooks in its own juices, with minimal added liquid required. Fish, which should always be scored to prevent bursting, vegetables and fruit are excellent cooked by either of these methods.

COOKING TECHNIQUES

For total success in microwave cooking, a number of simple operations, which do not usually apply to conventional cooking, need to be carried out.

Covering: This helps tenderize food and speed up cooking time by trapping steam. Recommended for vegetables, stews and for reheating food, except pies which would go soggy. Use a lid, inverted plate or microwave film, to allow some steam to escape. Cover bacon and sausages with paper towels to avoid splattering.

Stirring: Liquids and foods cut into pieces should be stirred to distribute heat evenly. Stir from the outside, where the food cooks first, towards the centre.

Turning: To avoid blind spots, which occur even in microwave cookers fitted with turntables or stirrer blades, dishes like joints or cakes, which cannot be stirred, should be rotated by a quarter or half turn during cooking. Joints of meat and poultry also need to be turned.

Arranging: Uneven-sized food, like chops, chicken drumsticks and small whole fish should be arranged with their thinner parts towards the centre of the dish where they will cook more slowly. Small food items, like scones, dumplings or fairy cakes, should be arranged in circles, and those on the outside moved to the centre during cooking.

Browning: Food may be browned under a conventional grill or in a browning dish, pre-heated according to the manufacturer's instructions; or use one of an increasing range of browning mixes specially developed for microwave cooking, or follow the suggestions under individual cooking methods.

Shielding: Cover protruding bones with tiny pieces of foil to prevent them from burning. Covering the foil with microwave film will afford your microwave cooker extra protection.

Piercing: Food with a skin or surface membrane such as jacket potatoes, sausages, chicken livers, egg yolks and tomatoes, must be pricked with a fork or cocktail stick to release pressure and prevent bursting. Fish and baked apples must be scored.

Standing: Food continues to cook by the conduction of heat after microwaving. It should be left to stand, covered, for the time specified in the recipe, to allow for the completion of cooking. This applies specially to joints of meat, cakes and puddings.

Turning

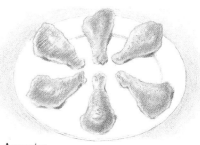

Arranging

Covering

Shielding

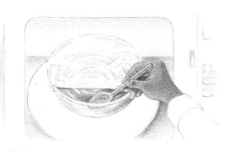

Stirring

Standing

COOKING FOR HEALTH

Less salt, less fat, less sugar – these golden rules of healthy eating are particularly easy to follow the microwave way. Salt attracts moisture so should not be used in microwave cooking as the food tends to dry out and toughen. Microwaved meat is juicy and tender with minimal added fat or oil; low-fat fish and chicken cook to perfection in the microwave cooker, as do fresh vegetables and wholefoods such as grains and wholewheat pasta. Fresh fruit can be stewed or poached in its own juice, with little added sugar.

Steaming, the most successful microwave cooking method, is also the best way to retain natural goodness. Food cooks so fast when microwaved that there is little time for valuable nutrients to be lost, and no wastage as there is no need for draining. Water-soluble and heat-sensitive vitamins survive much better when microwaved than in conventional cooking.

MICROWAVE AND FREEZER

The microwave-freezer combination is invaluable for impromptu meals, economical family batch-cooking and cook-ahead entertaining alike.

Thawing: Microwave cookers feature a defrost control which thaws food automatically, giving it a short burst of microwave energy followed by a rest period; this process is then repeated. If your microwave cooker does not have a defrost control, you can ensure gentle, even thawing, and avoid part of the food starting to cook before the rest is fully thawed, by microwaving on full power for a series of 30-second bursts, with 1½-minute intervals; this allows the heat to spread by conduction during the 'off' phase.

During thawing, food should be turned, and items such as chops or steaks separated; fruit and vegetables should be shaken or forked apart, and liquids and semi-liquid dishes like stews stirred and broken up at the beginning of thawing. Food should be covered where necessary, and the exuded liquid drained off during thawing, to speed up the process. For extra crispness, cakes, bread and pastry should be thawed on paper towels on a microwave rack or an upturned bowl.

It is most convenient to freeze food to be thawed/and reheated in the microwave in containers that are both freezer- and microwave-proof. Freezer-to-microwave-to-table ware is ideal. However, if foil freezer containers are used, remember to transfer the food before placing it in the microwave. Remember, too, to remove any freezer bag metal ties and replace them with string or elastic bands. Frozen vegetables packed in freezer bags can be conveniently cooked in the microwave straight from the freezer, without thawing. The microwave also proves invaluable in blanching vegetables for the freezer.

Reheating: It is not for nothing that the microwave has been nicknamed the unfreezer. Frozen or thawed food, or indeed any cold food, reheats wonderfully fast in the microwave cooker: the process often takes less than 1 minute. Refer to the charts on pages 137-140 when thawing foods. It is important to watch food very carefully when reheating. Most food should be reheated on full power and is ready when the container base feels hot. Stews, casseroles and frozen dishes are best microwaved initially on full power, then on low power for the second half of reheating time. All the cooking techniques described on page 132 apply to reheating.

Sliced meat and fibrous vegetables like broccoli and asparagus are best heated in a sauce. Whole meals on plates are easily reheated when stacked on special microwave plate rings (page 130). Pastry and bread should be reheated on paper towels, ideally elevated on a microwave rack or inverted bowl, to prevent sogginess.

CLEANING

Because microwaves do not radiate heat, the cooker walls do not become hot and spillages will not burn on as in a conventional oven so wiping down with a warm soapy cloth is all that is needed. This should be done frequently, ideally after each use. Attention should be paid to the door seal, which must be kept scrupulously clean to operate effectively. Never use abrasive cleaners. Boiling a cup of water in the microwave helps remove any stubborn food particles.

MICROWAVE SAFETY

Microwave cookers are produced to the most stringent specifications and have a number of built-in safety measures: for example, the microwaves can only be produced if the door is fully closed, and the doors are fitted with special locks, seals and safety cut-out switches. However, a few extra precautions may be taken:

- Choose a model carrying the BEAB (British Electrotechnical Approvals Board) guarantee of compliance with the British Standard for electrical safety and microwave leakage levels.
- The cavity may be damaged if the cooker is accidentally turned on while empty, so keep a cup of water in the oven when not in use.

- Never allow metal of any kind to come into contact with the oven cavity.
- Make sure the air vents above or behind the cooker are kept uncovered.
- Never tamper with or attempt to repair the microwave controls.
- Arrange for your cooker to be checked yearly by a qualified microwave service engineer.

MICROWAVE STANDBYS

JACKET POTATO

SERVES 1
1×175-225 g (6-8 oz) baking potato
butter
grated cheese

Wash, scrub and dry the potato, then prick all over with a fork. Place on paper towels and cook on Full/Maximum for 4-5 minutes, turning once during cooking, until soft when squeezed. Serve topped with butter and grated cheese.

WHITE SAUCE

MAKES 300 ml (½) pint
25 g (1 oz) butter or margarine, diced
25 g (1 oz) plain flour
300 ml (½ pint) milk
salt
white pepper

Put all the ingredients in a measuring jug and blend well. Cook on Full/Maximum for 4-5 minutes, whisking at 1-minute intervals, until the sauce has thickened. Adjust the seasoning, if necessary.

SCRAMBLED EGGS

SERVES 2
4 eggs
60 ml [4 tablespoons] milk
salt
freshly ground black pepper
25 g (1 oz) butter, diced
hot buttered toast, to serve

Using a balloon whisk, whisk the eggs with the milk in a medium bowl. Season with salt and pepper and add the butter. Cook on Full/Maximum for 1½ minutes, then whisk well. Cook on Full/Maximum for a further 1-1½ minutes, whisking well at 30-second intervals, until the eggs are light and creamy (they will continue to cook slightly after they are removed from the oven). Serve on hot buttered toast.

MICROWAVE COOKING TIPS

- Cover bacon and sausages cooked in a browning dish with paper towels to avoid splattering.
- In egg cookery, always prick whole yolks.
- Never attempt to boil eggs; they will burst.
- Use to melt chocolate without added water.
- Cook citrus fruit on Full/Maximum for 15-20 seconds to make squeezing and extraction of maximum juice easier.
- Do not grease or flour containers for cakes.
- Toasted nuts: microwave 75 g (3 oz) shelled nuts on Full/Maximum for 5-7 minutes, stirring from time to time.
- Dried herbs: place clean, dry fresh herbs between sheets of paper towels and cook on Full/Maximum for 3-4 minutes, turning once, then crush and store in airtight container.
- Use herbs and spices with care in microwave cooking, which brings out their full flavour.

MICROWAVE COOKING TIMES

FRESH VEGETABLES

Fresh vegetables and weight	Preparation	Water to be added	Approx. cooking time on full/maximum
Artichokes, 4 medium	Wash and trim	150 ml (¼ pint)	10-20 mins.
Aubergines 450 g (1 lb)	Peel and dice	2 tablespoons	5-6 mins.
Beetroot 450 g (1 lb)	Wash, skin and cut in half	None	7-8 mins.
Broad beans 450 g (1 lb)	Remove from pods and wash	2 tablespoons	7-10 mins.
Broccoli 225 g (8 oz)	Prepare, slice into spears	3 tablespoons	4-5 mins.
Brussels sprouts 225 g (8 oz)	Trim	3-4 tablespoons	7-8 mins.
Cabbage 450 g (1 lb)	Trim and shred	3 tablespoons	7-8 mins.
Carrots 225 g (8 oz)	Scrape and slice	2 tablespoons	6-7 mins.
Cauliflower 450 g (1 lb)	Trim and cut in florets	4 tablespoons	9-10 mins.
Celery, 1 head	Trim and dice	150 ml (¼ pint)	10-13 mins.
Corn on the cob (2)	Trim and wash	4 tablespoons	7-8 mins.
Courgettes 450 g (1 lb)	Trim, slice, sprinkle lightly with salt	None	7-9 mins.
Fennel 450 g (1 lb)	Slice	2 tablespoons	9-10 mins.
Leeks 450 g (1 lb)	Trim and slice	3 tablespoons	7-9 mins.
Mushrooms, button 100 g (4 oz)	Peel or wash, leave whole	2 tablespoons	2½-3 mins.
Onions 225 g (8 oz)	Peel and slice	2 tablespoons	4-6 mins.
Parsnips 450 g (1 lb)	Peel and slice	3 tablespoons	6-8 mins.
Peas 225 g (8 oz)	Remove from pods and wash	3 tablespoons	6-8 mins.
Potatoes, boiled 450 g (1 lb)	Peel and cut into evenly sized pieces	3 tablespoons	6-7 mins.
Potatoes, jacket (2) 225-275 g (8 oz-10 oz)	Scrub and prick well	None	9 mins.
Potatoes, sweet 450 g (1 lb)	Wash and prick well	2 tablespoons	5 mins.
Runner beans 225 g (8 oz)	String and slice	4 tablespoons	6-7 mins.
Spinach 225 g (8 oz)	Wash and shred	None	6-8 mins.
Swede 225 g (8 oz)	Peel and dice	None	6-8 mins.
Tomatoes 225 g (8 oz)	Slice	None	2-3 mins.
Turnips 225 g (8 oz)	Peel and dice	2 tablespoons	6-7 mins.

MICROWAVE COOKING TIMES

JOINTS OF MEAT

Joint and weight	Approx cooking time per 450 g (1 lb) on full/maximum	Standing time (wrapped tightly in foil)
Beef: 450 g (1 lb)	Rare: 4-5 mins. Medium: 7 mins. Well done: 9 mins.	20-30 mins.
Lamb: 450 g (1 lb)	7-9 mins.	25-30 mins.
Pork: 450 g (1 lb)	7-9 mins.	20-25 mins.
Gammon joints: 450 g (1 lb)	7 mins.	15-20 mins.
Chicken: 450g (1 lb)	6-7 mins.	15-20 mins.
Turkey: up to 3.5 kg (8 lb)	6-7 mins.	25-30 mins.

FISH

Fish and weight	Approx cooking time on full/maximum (cook, covered)	Standing time (covered)
Cod Fillets and Steaks 450 g (1 lb)	4 mins.	5-10 mins.
Plaice, gutted and filleted 450 g (1 lb)	3 mins.	5-10 mins.
Sole, filleted 450 g (1 lb)	3-4 mins.	5-10 mins.
Haddock, gutted and filleted 450 g (1 lb)	3 mins.	5-10 mins.
Mackerel (2), gutted but whole 225 g/8 oz	2 mins. each side	5-10 mins.
Kipper Fillets 225 g/8 oz	3 mins.	5 mins.

SMALL CUTS OF MEAT

Cut or type of meat and weight	Special points	Approx. cooking time on full/maximum	Standing time (covered)
Mince: 450 g (1 lb)	Cook covered	5 mins.	2 mins.
Steak: Rump or Fillet 225 g (8 oz)		3-4 mins.	2 mins.
Chops, loin: Lamb or Pork 2 portions 150 g (5 oz) each		6 mins.	2 mins.
Fillet: Lamb or Pork 350 g (12 oz)	Cook covered	6 mins.	5 mins.
Breast of Lamb: 560 g (1 lb 4 oz)	Cook on roasting rack.	6 mins.	3 mins.
Bacon: 225 g (8 oz)	Cook on rack	4 mins.	2 mins.
Chicken: 2 portions 400 g (14 oz) each	Cook on a rack to allow fat to drain. Sprinkle with browning agent	10 mins.	10-15 mins.
Gammon steaks: 2 portions 200 g (7 oz) each	Cook covered	2½-3 mins.	5 mins.
Gammon joints: 450 g (1 lb)	Cook covered	7 mins.	10 mins.
Liver: 450 g (1 lb)		4 mins.	5 mins.
Kidneys: 2 or 3	Slice before cooking	3-5 mins.	5 mins.

SPECIAL POINT FOR ALL MEAT: Meat cooking temperatures are calculated per pound weight.

MICROWAVE DEFROSTING TIMES

	JOINTS OF MEAT	
Type	Approximate time per 450 g (1 lb) on LOW setting	Special instructions
BEEF		
Boned roasting joints (sirloin, topside)	8-10 mins.	Turn over regularly during thawing and rest if the meat shows signs of cooking. Stand for 1 hour.
Joints on bone (rib of beef)	10-12 mins.	Shield bone end with small, smooth pieces of foil and overwrap with cling film. Turn the joint during thawing. The meat will still be icy in the centre but will thaw completely if you leave it to stand for 1 hour.
Minced beef	8-10 mins.	Stand for 10 mins.
Cubed steak	6-8 mins.	Stand for 10 mins.
Steak (sirloin, rump)	8-10 mins.	Stand for 10 mins.

Beefburgers
    standard (50 g (2 oz)
 	
    quarter-pounder
 	
    burger buns
	2 burgers: 2 mins.
	4 burgers: 2-3 mins.
	2 burgers; 2-3 mins.
	4 burgers: 5 mins.
	2 buns: 2 mins.
		Can be cooked from frozen, without thawing, if preferred.
		
		Stand burger buns for 2 mins.

PORK AND BACON		
Boned rolled joint (loin, leg)	7-8 mins.	As for boned roasting joints of beef above. Stand for 1 hour.
On the bone (leg, hand)	7-8 mins.	As for beef joints on bone above. Stand for 1 hour.
Tenderloin	8-10 mins.	Stand for 10 mins.
Chops	8-10 mins.	Separate during thawing and arrange 'spoke' fashion. Stand for 10 mins.
Bacon rashers	2 mins. per 225 g (8 oz)	Remove from pack; separate after thawing. Stand for 6-8 mins.

MICROWAVE DEFROSTING TIMES

LAMB/VEAL

Boned rolled joint (loin, leg, shoulder)	5-6 mins.	As for boned roasting joints of beef above. Stand for 30-45 mins.
On the bone (leg and shoulder)	5-6 mins.	As for beef joints on bone above. Stand for 30-45 mins.
Minced lamb or veal	8-10 mins.	Stand for 10 mins.
Chops	8-10 mins.	Separate during thawing. Stand for 10 mins.

OFFAL

Liver	8-10 mins.	Separate during thawing. Stand for 5 mins.
Kidney	6-9 mins.	Separate during thawing. Stand for 5 mins.

FISH

Type	Approximate time per 450 g (1 lb) on LOW setting	Special instructions
White fish fillets or cutlets, eg, cod, coley, haddock, halibut, or whole plaice or sole	3-4 mins. per 450 g (1lb), plus 2-3 mins.	Stand for 5 mins. after each 2-3 mins.
Oily fish, eg, whole and gutted mackerel, herring, trout	2-3 mins. per 225 g (8 oz) plus 3-4 mins.	Stand for 5 mins. after each 2-3 mins. and for 5 mins. afterwards.
Lobster tails, crab claws, etc	3-4 mins. per 225 g (8 oz), plus 2-3 mins.	As for oily fish above.
Crabmeat	2-3 mins. per 225 g (8 oz), plus 2-3 mins.	As for oily fish above.
Prawns, shrimps, scampi	2½ mins. per 100 g (4 oz) 3-4 mins. per 225 g (8 oz)	Pierce plastic bag, if necessary. Stand for 2 mins. Separate with a fork after 2 mins. Stand for 5 mins. then plunge into cold water and drain.

MICROWAVE DEFROSTING TIMES

POULTRY AND GAME

Type	Approximate time on LOW setting	Special instructions
Whole chicken or duckling	6-8 mins.	Remove giblets. Stand in cold water for 30 mins.
Whole turkey	10-12 mins.	Remove giblets. Stand in cold water for 2-3 hours.
Chicken portions	5-7 mins	Separate during thawing. Stand for 10 mins.
Poussin, grouse, pheasant, pigeon, quail	5-7 mins.	

BAKED FOODS

Type	Quantity	Approximate time on LOW setting	Special instructions
BREAD			
Loaf, whole Loaf, whole	1 large 1 small	6-8 mins. 4-6 mins.	Uncover and place on absorbent kitchen paper. Turn over during thawing. Stand for 5-15 mins.
Loaf, sliced Loaf, sliced	1 large 1 small	6-8 mins. 4-6 mins.	Defrost in original wrapper but remove any metal tags. Stand for 10-15 mins.
Slice of bread	25 g (1 oz)	10-15 seconds	Place on absorbent paper towels. Time carefully. Stand for 1-2 mins.
Bread rolls, tea cakes, scones	2 4	15-20 seconds 25-35 seconds	Place on absorbent paper towels. Time carefully. Stand for 2-3 mins.
Crumpets	2	15-20 seconds	Place on absorbent paper towels. Time carefully. Stand for 2-3 mins.
Croissants	2	15-20 seconds	Place on absorbent paper towels. Time carefully. Stand for 2-3 mins.

MICROWAVE DEFROSTING TIMES

CAKES AND PASTRIES

Cakes	2 small	30-60 seconds	Place on absorbent paper towels.
	4 small	1-1½ mins.	Stand for 5 mins.
Sponge cake	450 g (1 lb)	1-1½ mins.	Place on absorbent paper towels. Test and turn after 1 min. Stand for 5 mins.
Jam doughnuts	2	45-60 seconds	Place on absorbent paper towels.
	4	45-90 seconds	Stand for 5 mins.
Cream doughnuts	2	45-60 seconds	Place on absorbent paper towels. Check after half the thawing time.
	4	1¼-1¾ mins.	Stand for 10 mins.
Cream éclairs	2	45 seconds	Stand for 5-10 mins.
	4	1-1½ mins.	Stand for 15-20 mins.
Choux buns	4 small	1-1½ mins.	Stand for 20-30 mins.

PASTRY

| Shortcrust and puff | 225 g (8 oz) packet 1 min. | Stand for 20 mins. |
| | 400 g (14 oz) packet 2 mins. | Stand for 20-30 mins. |

INDEX

ACKNOWLEDGEMENTS

Photographer
HOWARD ALLMAN

Photographic styling
MARIAN PRICE

Preparation of food for photography
ANNE HILDYARD and LYNN
RUTHERFORD

Illustrations
JANE BREWSTER

Step by step illustrations
PATRICIA CAPON

Cover Photograph
VERNON MORGAN

Preparation of food for cover photograph
ALLYSON BIRCH

The publishers would also like to thank Moulinex Ltd, Sharp Electronics (UK) Ltd and
Thorn EMI Ltd for their kindness in lending microwave cookers to prepare food for
photography and for use in the photograph on page 2.